Pflichtmaterialien Abitur Niedersachsen 2025

Contents

Module III Greetings from Bury Park

Module IV A Midsummer Night's Dream

Contents

Module V Founder

Module VI Boy Erased

Info boxes (in alphabetical order)

Abbreviations and symbols

adj	adjective			
c.	*circa*, approximately	**p., pp.**	page, pages
cf.	compare, refer to	**par**	paragraph
f./ff.	and the following page(s)/line(s)	**pl**	plural
fml	formal	**sb.**	somebody
infml	informal	**sl**	slang
jdn., jdm.	*jemanden, jemandem*	**sth.**	something
l., ll.	line, lines	**v**	verb
n	noun		

▯▶ cornelsen.de
+◁᾽ Code: xxxxx

The webcode can be entered at *www.cornelsen.de* to connect you directly to a website with additional material.

◁᾽) Listening task (audio available)

▶ Viewing task (video available)

African American Experiences

Part A
Pre-reading activities

A1 Working with vocabulary

1 a Write down your own definition of the following terms. You may use a dictionary for help. Don't forget **F** and **G** on the next page.

A bias: _____

B prejudice: _____

C discrimination: _____

D identity: _____

E diversity: _____

F race: _____

G ethnicity: _____

  b Create a mind map to show connections between the words. Add
     at least five new words to your map.

A2 'I, Too' *Langston Hughes*

Read the poem 'I, Too' on the following page and complete the tasks
that follow.

I, too, sing America.

I am the darker brother.
They send me to eat in the kitchen
When company comes,
5 But I laugh,
And eat well,
And grow strong.

Tomorrow,
I'll be at the table
10 When company comes.
Nobody'll dare

Say to me,
'Eat in the kitchen,'
Then.

15 Besides,
They'll see how beautiful I am
And be ashamed–

I, too, am America.

*Photo of Langston
Hughes taken by
Nickolas Muray in
the 1920s.*

From: The Collected Works Vol. 1, Poems 1921–1940. University of Missouri Press, 2001.

Comprehension
1 Summarize the main idea of the poem in one or two sentences.

Analysis
2 Analyse the speaker's perspective (→ Info box, p. 158).
3 Examine the language used in the poem.
4 Describe the atmosphere at the end of the poem.

Beyond the text
5 Writing Langston Hughes wrote the poem 'I, Too' at the beginning of the 20th century
while still under the impression of segregation and Jim Crow. In groups, create a short 21st
century poem on the topic of race in the USA or Germany. You can refer to contemporary
events and developments (e.g. the Black Lives Matter movement).

Part B
While-reading activities

B1 'Cicada' *Camille Acker*

1 **a** Do some online research about cicadas.
   b Speaking Present your findings in a two-minute talk.
2 **a** In small groups, create a placemat on the topic of
   competition. In the area of the placemat in front of you,
   each answer the following questions:
   – Are you a competitive person? If so, in which areas of
     your life (sports, school, hobbies, appearance, etc.)?
   – What does it take to win a competition?
   – How do you cope if you don't win?
   b Slowly turn the placemat and read everyone's answers. Can you
   agree on some ideas? Present your results to the class.

Read the short story 'Cicada' by Camille Acker and complete the tasks
on pp. 20–23.

In the dank of DC's summer heat, cicadas scaled the heights of oak trees,
vocal and untrained trapeze artists. But their shells, discarded and
crumpled like candy wrappers, clogged drains and littered the sides of
the road. The air was smeared with humidity, but as they drove through
5 Rock Creek Park, a breeze lifted and Ellery, her face thrust out of the
car window, waited for the wind to hopscotch across her cheeks.
    'Stop'. Her mother tugged on Ellery's elbow and Ellery lowered her
face back into the interior of Ms. Anita's car.
    'Lo, she's fine.' Her father turned around from the passenger seat.
10 He frowned at her mother and winked at Ellery.
    'All these damn bugs. Devils, I tell you,' Ms. Anita said. The wheels
of her car crushed the dark masses again and again.
    On the playground at Ellery's school, a boy picked up one of the
cracked bodies and threw it at the long, full ponytail of a girl. She tried
15 to shake free of it, catching the Holy Ghost far from the aisles of any
church, like the one Ellery's mother dragged her to on Sundays. 'Get it
out! Get it off!' the girl yelled. The giggling bunch of boys ran, but Ellery,
with her thumb and forefinger, pulled the bug remains out of the strands
of hair.
20   'My science teacher says they wait underground until they're ready
to come out,' Ellery said. She tried to lean forward between the seats,
but the seat belt pulled her back.

1 dank [dæŋk]: damp
1 cicada [sɪˈkɑːdə]:
Heuschrecke
2 vocal: loud
2 discarded: thrown away
3 clog (v): block
6 hopscotch (v): jump
irregularly
8 interior: inside
18 remains (n, pl): what
is left of sth.

'Your dress,' her mother said. She brushed non-existent bits of lint from the fabric, stiff from the dry cleaning. Her mother had insisted
25 that would make it look best for today. It didn't smell like it had been cleaned, not like their clothes after they washed them at the laundromat. Their dryer at home had been broken since last summer. Their washing machine had stopped at Christmas.

'You go all this way for her to take piano?' Ms. Anita asked. 'I bet
30 there's somebody right over in Northeast.'

'You're probably right, Ms. Anita,' Mom answered back. She had to yell so her voice would land on the waiting ears of Ms. Anita instead of the wind taking it out to the trees.

'Too much money over here, you ask me,' Ms. Anita said.
35 'Appreciate this ride, especially today. All of these rides you've given us. We could have taken the bus –'

'Probably have to take two different ones to get you this far west of the park.'

'Three,' her mother said, but this time she did not yell.
40 The kids in her neighborhood all hated being west of the park: Woodley Park of Friendship Heights or Ellery's favorite neighborhood (the site of her piano lessons, the site of today's excitement), the Gold Coast. Ellery had no name for the collection of streets around her home where she skinned knees and hands. The houses on the Gold Coast
45 weren't just in rows, obedient toy soldiers. These houses were like gathering up all the toys Ellery had ever owned, the Barbies, the stuffed animals, the building blocks. They had what her mother called Turrets of Juliet balconies and front yards big enough for a good game of tag. Even the plain brick ones caused a tightness in Ellery's belly. Some of
50 them had ivy growing up the sides, angling for a way in.

'I don't know how you've been making it without a car –'

'We've been making it fine,' her father said.

'Even to the Gold Coast?' Ms. Anita asked. Her father said that Ms. Anita wouldn't believe you even if you said water was wet. When Ellery
55 went over to use Ms. Anita's piano to practice, she would always ask how long it'd be. 'Just an hour, Ms. Anita,' her mother told her. 'About the same time it would take me to do your hair.' And then, Ms. Anita, putting a hand to her gelled ponytail, would say, 'Well, if it's just an hour…'
60 'Mom, look,' Ellery said. 'I bet it's cold in there.' She reached out to grip her mother's forearm without turning to see where her fingers would land. Ellery could feel drops of sweat down her back like her mother pouring water over her head in the kitchen sink when she got her hair washed, the towel on her neck already good and soaked. The
65 wetness now the stickiness of salt, not the stickiness of conditioner.

'So, this a recital?' Ms. Anita asked. She watched for the answer in her rearview mirror waiting for Ellery's mother to respond.

23 lint: *Fussel*
26 laundromat: *SB-Waschsalon*
44 skin sth. (v): *sich etw. abschürfen*
45 obedient: doing what so. ordered you to do
47 Turrets of Juliet: reference to scene in Romeo and Juliet in which Juliet speaks to Romeo from the balcony
48 tag (n): *Fangen (Spiel)*
50 ivy: *Efeu*
64 soaked: very wet
66 recital: concert

'No it's a competition. Mrs. Hamilton says that's like a recital with prizes,' Ellery answered before her mother could.

70 'Oh yeah? You gonna win?' Ms. Anita asked. She jutted an elbow out to Ellery's father and smiled.

'Yes,' Ellery said. When she played the piano, Ellery could find no edges to the world, no start and stop. Not in the music or in the Italian words Mrs. Hamilton used to tell Ellery to slow down or play loudly. The 75 world was there for her. She was just waiting to come out and see it.

* * *

Ms. Anita's car clunked into the circular driveway of the recital hall. It was really a kind of church, a synagogue, her father told them.

'Pretty slick, huh?' Dad said. But Ellery wouldn't have called the building slick, not like the shine on the escalators in the Metro. The 80 white building trimmed in the silver of its four large columns was more like the platter they used for Thanksgiving and Christmas dinner. Ellery was never allowed to carry it to the table or even pick it up when she served herself turkey. Ms. Anita rounded the corners of the drive and braked her old car in front of the large wooden doors of the synagogue. 85 The cicadas were quieter here.

'Ready?' her father asked. He craned around to smile at Ellery in the back seat. The armpits of his white shirt were already soaked through with sweat. Her mother rubbed her back and Ellery nodded.

'You sure you won't come, Ms. Anita?' Mom asked.

90 'Got my book club,' Ms. Anita said. 'But you call me and I'll come back.'

Her father opened the car door and Ellery climbed out, trying to keep her legs together like her mother always said, but she couldn't get out of the car like that. She jumped out and landed with a hop on the 95 sidewalk. She made sure not to turn in case disapproval was on her mother's face. Her father grabbed one of her hands, her mother the other, and they walked toward the building. Ms. Anita's car creaked away behind them.

The four doors before them were the dark wood of the banister at 100 Grandma's house that Mom always told her was not meant for messing. Glass above the wood reflected their three bodies back to them, but it would have taken at least six Ellerys stacked on one another for her to reach the top. In the white stone above the glass, somebody had carved two candleholders and one picture of a book with round corners instead 105 of pointy ones. It was better than any Gold Coast house she'd ever seen. Her father tugged at her hand to get her through one of the doors.

Inside, the ceilings stretched even higher than the glass. It would take even more Ellerys to reach the top. Her shoes echoed on the synagogue's stone floor: each sole striking as if someone were bouncing 110 a ball.

70 jut sth. out: stick sth. out
76 clunk (v): make a dull sound
78 slick [slɪk] (adj): smart, cool
80 trimmed: *umrandet*
81 platter ['plætə(r)]: *Servierteller*
86 crane (v): stretch
97 creak (v): *quietschen*
99 banister ['bænɪstə(r)]: railing
100 messing (n, infml): playing about
103 carve sth.: *schnitzen*
105 pointy: sharp and spiked

'Sure feels nice in here,' Dad said. He wiped his brow with his free hand.

The outstretched arms of smiling women with flowers pinned to the front of their clothes directed them to a red carpeted area in front of
115 more doors. Now, Ellery's shoes couldn't be heard at all, as if she had vanished. There was just one door this time, wide and wooden. Her father grabbed a silver handle and opened it for Ellery to walk through. Her mother held her hand even tighter as if they were about to cross the street.

120 At the front of this new room, the one where she would perform, was the same rounded book, but bigger and lit up, maybe from a spotlight somewhere Ellery couldn't see. Ellery and her mother belonged to a congregation that was small and, as her father said, too broke to worship anywhere better than a high school cafeteria. The sanctuary
125 was a bunch of metal folding chairs and tables that sometimes had dried ketchup on them. It always smelled of newly opened cans of corn.

Here, the air was like right after her mother vacuumed the carpet. There were no worn-out tables, the ones at the front too beautiful for anybody to ever be allowed to get ketchup near them. Four steps led
130 up to the stage, glowing from the light of the big book and from the gleam of polished wood. To the left side was all that mattered, a piano: grand, white, and gleaming. It was not the old upright at Ms. Anita's or the kind at Mrs. Hamilton's, smaller than this one and black.

Mrs. Hamilton descended from her place on the stage. Her long
135 brown hair was piled on the top of her head in a bun. Ellery's mother wore her hair in a bun like that sometimes, but only when she didn't care what her hair looked like. At the stove when she was cooking. When they carried laundry baskets full of clothes to the laundromat. Mrs. Hamilton wasn't about to do laundry or cook a pot of spaghetti.
140 Her hair was messy on purpose. And even though her dress sparkled, golden threads woven into the swirls of deep pink and white, Mrs. Hamilton didn't look dressed up.

'And you're here,' Mrs. Hamilton said. Even words that weren't Italian Mrs. Hamilton said as though they were. She had lived in Europe,
145 she told Ellery often. All over Europe. One place in Europe would have been plenty for Ellery, but that it was more than one seemed important to Mrs. Hamilton. Mrs. Hamilton shook Mom's and Dad's hands, clasping their one hand with both of hers, ringed and nail polished. 'The parents may sit anywhere they like. Closer is better of course to see the beautiful
150 finger work Signorina Ellery will do.'

Her father scanned the half-filled cushioned movie theater seats. 'Space right there.' He grabbed Ellery's shoulder and shook it. 'You'll do great.'

'It'll be beautiful. I already know,' her mother said. She fished for a
155 comb in her purse and fussed over the front of Ellery's hair. She leaned

116 vanish: disappear
123 congregation
[ˌkɒŋɡrɪˈɡeɪʃn]: *Gemeinde*
123 broke (infml): having no money
124 sanctuary: *Altarraum*
127 vacuum sth.
[ˈvækjuːm] (v): hoover sth.
131 gleam (n): shine
132 upright (n): (here) standing piano
135 bun: (here) *Dutt*
141 swirl (n): round pattern
147 clasp sb./sth. (v): grip sb./sth.

back to check her work and smiled. Baby powder peeked out from the neckline of her mother's black dress. If Ellery touched it, the whiteness would only spread.

160   Her father jingled the change in his pocket. 'Come on, we don't want to lose those seats.'

    Her mother stroked Ellery's hair again. Dad put a hand on her back and led her away.

    'Shall we meet your competition?' Mrs. Hamilton said.

    The other students, some boys, mostly girls, were seated in the first
165 row. A few of them only nodded at her as Mrs. Hamilton went down the line naming those she knew and prompting others to introduce themselves. 'Have a seat here.' Mrs. Hamilton gestured to an empty seat between two girls, both in cropped, colorful sweaters and spring dresses. Both had stud earrings, and one, when she touched a hand to her
170 tortoiseshell headband, revealed a silver bracelet with a tiny silver tag hanging from it. They sat with their ankles crossed and their hands picking at starched sundress collars. These girls got out of cars with their legs together and their shoes unscuffed.

    'I'm Cara,' the girl without the bracelet said when Ellery sat down.
175 She wasn't nearly as pretty as the other girl. Mrs. Hamilton clicked away from them in her high heels.

    'I'm Ellery,' she said. She turned to smile at the other girl too, the one with the bracelet, even though she hadn't yet given her name.

    'I like your hair,' the girl said. She pulled on her blond ponytail,
180 resting it on her shoulder.

    Ellery's hair had been pressed that morning. She had begged her mother for months to let her cut it. She would be in junior high soon, she told her, couldn't she be just a little grown now? Her mother finally cut it when she knew Ellery would be in the competition. Ellery felt the
185 ends of her hair and smiled at her.

    'I wish my hair were fuller like that. Mine is so fine and lays so flat, but you've got that kind of poof at your roots.' The girl widened her eyes when she said *poof*.

    Ellery nodded. She felt an ache somewhere her arms were too short
190 to reach.

    'Lori!' Cara whisper-shouted before she let escape a small laugh. Her voice snapped to pity when Ellery's hand went to the front of her hair. 'She's just like that,' Cara assured her.

    Lori probably cheated at war and ate all the red Now and Laters in
195 the pack. Lori might have lived in one of those houses that Ellery loved, but she wouldn't last one minute with an alley-glass-skinned knee. She'd have gone home crying to her mother. She wouldn't have gotten right back on her bike and kept riding.

159 jingle sth. ['dʒɪŋgl] (v): *etw. klimpern*
166 prompt sb./sth. to do sth. [prɒmpt]: *dazu bringen*
169 stud earring [stʌd 'ɪərɪŋ]: *Ohrstecker*
170 tortoiseshell ['tɔːtəsʃel]: *Schildpatt*
171 ankle: *Knöchel*
172 starched [staːtʃt]: stiff
173 unscuffed [ʌn'skʌft]: undamaged
194 Now and Later: brand of sweets

One of the other white women besides Mrs. Hamilton quieted the
200 crowd. Her fingers pressed down on the air as if she were playing all
the keys of the piano at once.

Ellery turned to search for the faces of her parents, but she could no
longer tell, even in the swarm of white bodies, which bodies she
belonged to. She thought she saw her mother's hair between the gelled
205 heads of two suited black men, but when she leaned her head back to
make sure, Lori hissed at her.

'Your teacher's looking at you. You better pay attention,' Lori said.
Ellery tilted forward, sitting straighter in her seat so she wouldn't
disappoint Mrs. Hamilton. When she glanced Mrs. Hamilton's way
210 though, she wasn't watching Ellery, only the stage. 'Maybe she was
looking somewhere else,' Lori said. She shrugged her shoulders.

Ellery placed her folded hands in her lap just like Lori and tried to hold
her knees together through the songs of the youngest kids, all of the
tunes short, in four-four time, and played allegro, joyful and fast.

215 Finally, Ellery's age group began to play. Each pianist (Mrs. Hamilton
said Ellery should call herself that) in their turn going up to the stage,
having their piece announced, and then setting off, waiting for their
fingers to remember all the movements that had been drilled into them
for weeks. Some of them had placed in competitions before, Mrs.
220 Hamilton told her at her lessons. But it didn't mean they were any better
than her and even those who had won had no advantage: 'Winning once
doesn't mean you will win again,' Mrs. Hamilton said.

Lori went up to play and Ellery let her knees go limp and her ankles
uncross. A woman announced the title of Lori's piece and before she
225 sat at the bench, Lori raised a shoulder and a smile for the audience,
who complimented this preperformance with louder applause than the
girl before her had received at the end of her song. From head to toe,
Lori was a new Mary Jane shoe fresh out of the box, buffed to a shine
so you could see your own reflection in it, but all lopsided and weird.
230 The squeeze and hurt of it. Still, Ellery also longed for pretty things.
She clapped, but with her hands still in her lap.

The Italian words resounded in Lori's playing. *Forte* when it should
be. *Piano* when it was best. Lori might really know those words, maybe
she had been all over Europe like Mrs. Hamilton. Lori's finger positioning
235 was precise, her hands arched as if tennis balls rested under her palms.
It was the way Mrs. Hamilton wanted Ellery to play, but Ellery's hands
sometimes fell a little flat, perched too low.

'Hey,' Cara said, poking Ellery's still-folded hands. From the side of
the stage, this time Mrs. Hamilton *was* looking at her and motioning
240 with both hands for Ellery to come. Standing, Ellery would have the
best chance to see her parents, but looking behind her might mean
tripping over something. She walked towards Mrs. Hamilton, never

201 key: (here)
Klaviertaste
206 hiss at sb./sth. [hɪs]:
make a noise resembling
that of a snake at sb./sth.
208 tilt (v): lean
223 limp (adj): relaxed
228 Mary Jane shoe:
klassischer Spangenschuh
228 buffed [bʌft]:
polished
229 lopsided [ˌlɒpˈsaɪdɪd]:
schräg
232 resound in/through
sth. [rɪˈzaʊnd]:
widerhallen
235 arched: *gewölbt*
237 perched [pɜːtʃt]:
niedergelassen

turning around with her hands clasped in front of her.

245 'Go up and wait.' Mrs. Hamilton gently pushed at Ellery's back. She walked up three steps to the stage, concealed from the audience by velvet curtains. Ellery could focus on Lori's face now, the way she
250 couldn't sitting right next to her. Her nose was smaller than Ellery's. Her cheeks the pink of watermelon candy, a color that would have been muted on Ellery's dark skin. Lori's ponytail flounced as she played, as excited to be there with her as the rest of the audience was. She was pretty good,
255 but maybe church just made music better.

Sometimes on Sundays, Ellery's mother would raise a hand and wave it during a song. Once after service, Ellery asked her why she did that. All her mother would say is that she felt full. Ellery thought of the discomfort of too many hamburgers or one scoop too many of ice
260 cream, but her mother's full – a hand at her heart and the dots of tears at the corners of her eyes – was different. 'All I feel just comes out,' she told Ellery.

Lori finished, and when she rose from the bench and bowed, the audience clapped happily. Three people in the front wrote on sheets of
265 paper, the judges, she now remembered Mrs. Hamilton whispering to her on the walk to her seat. A row of well-dressed white people stood up, clapping louder than the rest. Lori exited the stage and came toward Ellery. Lori looked like she might speak, but only poked her lips out at Ellery and pulled her wandering ponytail back to its place on her
270 shoulder.

The woman announced Ellery's piece and extended her hand to invite Ellery to start playing. Ellery moved out of the shadows of the curtains and stood before the audience. She started to bow, but did it slowly hoping during her bending she would finally see her parents, but she
275 couldn't find them. She wasn't even sure where her own seat was anymore. The distance from her to the piano grew, but Ellery imagined this was Ms. Anita's house, the same shaky wooden bench, the same smell of bleach and Vaseline, her mother just starting on Ms. Anita's hair.

280 Ellery sat at the keys and placed the tips of her fingers on the ivories. She lightly stroked them. Then, she finally pressed down and played the opening chord. She loved the way it sounded. Her fingers raced across the keys to the next chord. *Too fast*, she hears Mrs. Hamilton say in her head as she would in practice. Ellery slowed and pressed each
285 note so every one would be heard. She chanted Italian words, whispering them to herself. Most had nothing to do with her song, but the melody of them made her want to do her best. The notes placed

248 velvet ['velvɪt]: *Samt*
253 flounce [flaʊns] (v): make exaggerated movements
268 poke sth. out at sb./ sth.: push sth. out at sb./ sth.
278 bleach (n): disinfectant made of chlorine
280 ivories (pl): (here) piano keys
285 chant (v): sing

well together, and those notes led to the new notes, which led to the other notes. Ellery didn't know if this piano was better or if this church,
290 this synagogue, where music played that made people feel full, was doing the same for her music, but she felt it. She felt full. Or maybe she felt just out of the dirt, out from underground and into the summer sun. She touched the last of the notes, her fingers light on them, *piano*, and then off of them and back into her lap.
295   She heard the clapping before she stood up all the way, before she turned around and took her bow. And then she saw them, her parents standing up like Lori's had. Her father yelling and calling out her name. Her mother wasn't clapping, but she had a hand to her heart. Cara was waiting to play and could only stare at Ellery. At the bottom of the
300 three stairs, Mrs. Hamilton leaned toward Ellery and touched the side of her face. 'Beautiful,' she told her. Ellery smiled. Some people were still clapping, some people who weren't even her parents. Ellery walked back to her seat. Lori didn't say anything, didn't even give her a smile. Ellery sat and Cara played, but even though the room was filled with as
305 much sound as before, Ellery heard nothing over the thump of her heartbeat.

* * *

They announced the winners for the younger kids first, the third prize and the second. The first-prize winner, a boy with blue pants, a pinstriped shirt, and a bowtie, ran up when they called his name. His parents took
310 pictures, and he smiled and posed until they said he could stop. The woman who had introduced all of them stepped back to the microphone after the little boy finally left the stage. She thanked everyone for coming and then began to thank a long list of other people.
    'You were really good,' Cara whispered to Ellery. Ellery smiled, but
315 didn't thank her, wary of daggers of giggles that might follow.
    'Any *thing* can make noise,' Lori said.
    'You were really good, like really good,' Cara said again without a giggle or a smile to diminish her words.
    'For our nine-to-twelve age group, we had some excellent
320 competitors representing many parts of the city. Our judges had a difficult task, but we chose three pianists we think excelled today.'
    She paused, and Ellery didn't want to hope too hard that her name would come out of her mouth. 'In third place and winning one hundred dollars, Bobby McMillan.'
325   From the other side of the crowd, a boy Ellery hadn't even remembered playing went up. He shook the woman's hand up and down and up and down until she took her hand away to give him two stiff pieces of paper, a certificate and a check.
    'And, in second place, with a piece that showed real technique by a
330 pianist who exhibited great poise – that's the importance of this

305 thump [θʌmp] (n): loud noise
308 pinstriped: *mit Nadelstreifen*
315 wary: not ready to trust
315 dagger ['dægə(r)]: *Dolch*; daggers of giggles ['gɪglz]: (here) being laughed at
318 diminish sb/sth.: belittle
330 poise (n): calm and confident manner

competition too, not just playing music, but turning these kids into true ladies and gentlemen.'

Ellery didn't know if she had been ladylike enough for this woman or if she had 'great poise'.

335   'Our second-place prize of two hundred fifty dollars goes to Lori Hansen.'

'See,' Lori breathed out before she went forward to claim her trophy and check. She curtsied for the audience and they clapped harder.

Lori came back to Ellery's side and hissed, 'Can't imagine you'll be
340   able to top that.'

'And our first-prize winner in our nine-to-twelve age group is someone who really surprised the judges…' The woman stopped, building urgency, and Ellery knew her mother was in the audience saying to her father, 'Why don't she get on with it?' Ellery wanted her
345   to, but then she didn't because she might not have won and then she would have to turn to this girl next to her and say something about her winning, not because she really wanted to, but because she would want her to know her parents had taught her well.

Ellery took in a deep breath to either help her say 'thank you' to the
350   judges or 'Congratulations' to Lori.

'The winner is Ellery Cook.'

Ellery heard a squeal from the audience. She walked up the steps of the stage and to the waiting woman. The fullness of playing multiplied, winning all the marbles in a game of jacks, seeing a tree full of cicadas
355   where it seemed at first there was just one. The trophy was just a note, a musical note, mounted on a stone stand, but on that stand were the words *First Place*. But what Ellery really wanted was the $500 check.

The woman smiled and handed it to her. 'Congratulations.'

Ellery didn't shake her hand like the boy had and she didn't curtsy.
360   Her smile and thank-you were so small, they ended up being only for herself. She descended the stairs of the stage to more congratulations and compliments on her playing. Everyone was standing up, kids finding their parents and parents finding their joyous or disappointed child.

Lori and Cara were just past the last step. Ellery fingered her first-
365   place trophy and Lori fingered the careful pleats of her dress.

'Winning is just for fun,' Lori said.

'It was fun,' Ellery said. 'How I won.'

The watermelon candy at Lori's cheeks darkened.

Out of clusters of people, Ellery's parents emerged. Her father
370   whooping and letting loose emphatic one-word sentences. 'Yes.' 'Right.' 'Winner.' Ellery could see from her mother's swollen eyes that she had been crying.

'This one,' Mrs. Hamilton said, floating toward them and pointing at Ellery, 'did magnificently well.'

338 curtsy ['kɜ:tsi]: (v) *knicksen*
343 urgency: (here) tension
352 squeal (n): high-pitched sound
354 marble: *Murmel*
365 pleat [pli:t]: *Falte*
370 emphatic: said with real feeling

Small ball and jacks used to play a game of jacks

375 'We thought so too,' Dad said. He patted Ellery's head, mussing her
hair until she allowed a smile to escape.

'It was so beautiful. The song,' her mother said. 'I've heard her play
it, but –'

'She played it better today than she ever has,' Mrs. Hamilton said.
380 'You like your prize?'

Ellery nodded, renewing her grip on the trophy. She moved away
from her parents so she could present the check. She wanted to do it
just like the lady on the lottery drawing. 'Here. It's for the car. We won't
have to take the bus,' Ellery said. She unfolded her arm and let the
385 peach-colored paper dangle from her fingertips.

Her mother glanced at Mrs. Hamilton and then squatted down in
front of Ellery. She placed her hand under one curled side of Ellery's
hair. 'Honey, it's a saving bond.'

The bond was stiffer than cash or a check, but Ellery didn't know
390 why that made a difference. She searched her father's face for the
answer.

'See, baby, that number it has? That five hundred? Well, it's worth
something it's not really worth yet. But by the time you go to college,
by then, what it says it's worth, it'll be worth,' her father said.

395 'Don't worry about a car. This is yours,' her mother said. She pushed
Ellery's hair behind her ear, only to pull it back out again. Grooming her
even though her moment was over.

'Oh.' Ellery dropped the hand with the bond down to her side.

'You kind of have to believe it'll get to be worth that in time,' her
400 father said. He put a hand on Mom's back and she straightened back to
her height. Ellery looked no one in the eye.

'You won, remember?' Mrs. Hamilton said, her voice in a sharp key.
'Smile.'

* * *

They waited in the circular driveway for Ms. Anita to come. From the
405 trees, the cicadas were deafening the street, before they would be gone
for seventeen more years. By then, Ellery would be grown and the $500
savings bond would finally be worth its face value. Her parents chattered
along with the cicadas. They told her how proud they were and how
beautiful her playing was. Mom couldn't wait to tell the other members
410 of the choir, and Dad couldn't wait to tell everybody he knew.

Lori and her family came out through the dark, wooden doors. Ellery
tightened her grip on the trophy and savings bond. The people who had
stood up and cheered for Lori surrounded her now. Two men in suits and
two ladies in grown-up versions of the dress Lori had on. The group walked
415 around Ellery's family, but Lori came closer than the others, brushing past
Ellery's mother, her pink cashmere cardigan nudging the polyester of her
mother's dress. Her mother turned toward Lori and her family.

375 muss (v): make
untidy
385 dangle from sth. (v):
hang loosely
386 squat [skwɒt] (v):
bend your knees and go
down
402 key: (here) *Tonart*
407 savings bond [bɒnd]:
Sparbrief
416 nudge sb./sth.
[nʌdʒ]: touch lightly

'Congratulations,' Lori said. The family members nodded their approval of Lori's word.

420 'Say thank you, Ellery,' her mother said. Ellery squeezed her mother's hand, but did not speak. Her mother smiled at Lori and found the faces of the adults. 'Your daughter. She was wonderful.'

'Yes, thank you.' The woman had Lori's face, but no watermelon candy at her cheeks. Hair that might once have been pulled into a 425 coveted ponytail lay on her shoulders, straightened and brightly blond. On one wrist was a bracelet with the small tag that Lori's had and a ring with a stone so far from her finger it seemed suspended in midair. Her dress looked as if it had been dry-cleaned. No sweat ringed her underarms. There was no baby powder to be found.

430 'That dress is very pretty,' her mother said. She always knew how much things cost without looking at price tags. 'Slow down,' she would tell Ellery, 'don't splash water on that lady,' she might say, 'that dress cost her good money.' 'Don't kick that dirt up around that man, his suit is more than I make in a week.'

435 'Thank you.' The woman took Lori's hand and turned away from Ellery's mother.

They walked to a car nearby, silver like the synagogue's columns. The car's horn beeped and one of the men opened the front door for the woman holding Lori's hand. The man opened the door for Lori next. Lori
440 turned back and smiled. Her teeth were so straight, white fence posts lined up and freshly painted. She smoothed out the back of her skirt and sat down. The man closed the door behind her and all Ellery could see of Lori through the window was the pink of her face and the blond of her ponytail.

445 'Now, that's a beautiful thing right there. Never seen that model in that color,' her father said. He leaned down and said very near Ellery's ear, 'One day soon, we'll be riding in that.'

Other car doors closed, slammed. The cicadas only got louder.

Lori's car started to take off, going around the circular driveway of
450 the synagogue. Ellery dropped her mother's hand and walked toward the departing car, quickening her steps when the wheels began to spin faster. When her legs couldn't keep up, she bent down and picked up the shells of the cicadas, pushed to the side in gutters and broken under indifferent wheels. She hurled the black bodies at the windows of the
455 car. She ran now, her Mary Janes pinching. She picked up more cicada shells, throwing two or three at a time and then three or four more. She threw all the shells she could find, even when the car pulled out of the driveway. She was breathing fast by the time she stopped running at the end of the drive, still holding a couple of cicada shells in her hand.
460 She walked back toward the synagogue, turning around as she went to see how far away the car was.

425 coveted ['kʌvətɪd]: very wanted
427 suspended: hanging in the air
453 gutter ['gʌtə(r)]: Gosse

'Did you see?' Ellery asked her parents. Ellery breathed out and smiled. 'Did you?'

From: Training School for Negro Girls, Feminist Press at the City University of New York, 2018, pp. 7–26.

> **Info Camille Acker**
> African American author Camille Acker was raised in Washington DC. She studied English and Creative Writing, which she has been teaching in different contexts. Her debut collection of short stories *Training School for Negro Girls* (2018), set in her hometown, is about the lives of young Black girls and women. Camille Acker now lives in Philadelphia and works as a writer, researcher and editor.

Comprehension

3 Answer the following questions with short answers:

a Where does the short story take place?

_____

b Why did Ellery's mother have to bring her daughter's dress to get dry-cleaned?

_____

c What seems to be the difference between the street Ellery lives on and the Gold Coast part of town?

_____

d Why does Ms Anita let Ellery use her piano?

_____

e What does Ellery try to do when leaving the car?

_____

f What is the difference between the first impression we get of Ellery and that of the other girls?

_____

g How does Ellery think Lori would get on if she had an accident like Ellery?

_____

h What impression does Ellery get of Lori playing?

_____

i What does Ellery first do when she feels nervous in front of the audience?

_____

j How does Ellery react when Cara compliments her on her performance?

_____

k How does Ellery react to Lori winning the second prize?

_____

l How does Lori react to Ellery winning the first prize?

_____

m What does Ellery want to do with her prize money and why is she disappointed?

_____

Analysis

4 Compare the synagogue with the church Ellery's family go to.

5 a From lines 13–19 Ellery is picking the cicada from the other girl's hair. How would you characterize her up to this point in the story? Pick at least three words from the box below or add your own. Use a dictionary if needed. Make sure to explain why you used the words you chose and give evidence from the text.

> brave · strong · timid · angry · friendly · well-behaved · ambitious · self-confident · shy · naïve · clever · arrogant · intimidating · driven

b Consider the rest of the story from this point until the end and come back to your answer from **a**. Add new aspects to your characterization of Ellery if necessary.

6 How would you translate Ellery's mother's statement that she 'feels full' (l. 256–262) into German?

7 Contrast how Ellery and Lori are presented in the story. Fill in the information in the table on the next page. You can add another category if needed.

Feature	Ellery	Lori
parents		
appearance		
clothing		
behaviour during the competition		
behaviour after the competition		
…		

8 Discuss how the story would change if Ellery were white and Lori Black. Would it still work in your opinion? Why or why not?

9 a Think of the typical structure of a short story. Look up the technical terms in the table below if you are not sure. Explain their usual function in the structure of a short story and point out where in 'Cicada' you can find them. Fill in the information in the table.

Stage	General function	in 'Cicada'
exposition		
rising action		
climax		
falling action		
resolution		

b Compare your answers with a partner and discuss your results.

Beyond the text

10 a Ellery's parents are shocked about her behaviour and demand an explanation when they arrive back at their apartment after the recital. Work in groups of three and prepare a role-play of the conversation.

b Speaking Act out your role-play in front of the class.

11 Writing After getting home, Ellery receives a text message from her best friend who wants to know how the recital went. Write her reply.

12 As a class, prepare a game of 'Good Angel – Bad Angel'. Split into two groups with one person portraying Ellery sitting between both groups. One group portrays the good angels, telling Ellery to continue and the other group portrays the bad angels who tell her to stop competing. Both groups give reasons for their advice. After both groups are finished giving their arguments, listen to Ellery make her choice.

B2 'Fatima, the Biloquist: A Transformation Story' *Nafissa Thompson-Spires*

1 a Brainstorm associations for the word 'transformation'. How would you define it and what would you expect from a 'transformation story'?
  b Work in groups around a placemat. One after the other, write down your results from **a** in your space on the placemat.
  c Share your results with the class.

Read the short story 'Fatima, the Biloquist: A Transformation Story' by Nafissa Thompson-Spires and complete the tasks on pp. 34–36.

There are happier stories one could tell about Fatima. In the nineties you could be whatever you wanted – someone said that on the news – and by 1998 Fatima felt ready to become black, full black, baa baa black sheep black, black like the elbows and knees on praying folk black, if
5 only someone would teach her.

Up to that point she had existed like a sort of colorless gas, or a bit of moisture, leaving the residue of something familiar, sweat stains on a T-shirt, hot breath on the back of a neck, condensation rings on wood, but never fullness of whatever matter had formed them.
10 The week she met Violet, Fatima had recited 'An Address to the Ladies, by their Best Friend Sincerity' before her eleventh-grade AP English class. She blended her makeup to perfection that morning, but the other students barely looked at her, instead busying themselves by clicking and replacing the lead in mechanical pencils
15 or folding and flicking paper footballs over finger goalposts – even during the part she recited with the most emphasis: 'Ah! sad, perverse, degenerate race / The monstrous head deforms the face.' They clapped dull palms for a few seconds as Fatima sulked back to her desk. But they sat up, alert, when Wally 'The Wigger' Arnett recited
20 'Incident' and said the word that always made the white kids pay attention.

'You know, I identify with Countee Cullen and all,' Wally, with brown freckles and a floppy brown haircut, finished up. 'He was a black man, and he was, like, oppressed for who he was and stuff.'

00 biloquist [bɪləkwɪst]: person who speaks with two voices
3 baa [bɑː]: noise sheep make in children's books
10 recite sth.: say sth. from memory
10 'An Address to the Ladies …': US poem written by Charles Brockden Brown (1771–1810), first published in 1788
20 'Incident': poem by African American writer Countee Cullen (1903–1946)

25 The hands pounded a hero's applause as Wally headed back to his seat next to Fatima looking like he expected a high five. She rolled her eyes at him, but she couldn't articulate her wrath into something more specific. Later that morning, when Wally asked her for the fourth time that semester whether she listened to No Limit rappers, 30 she lunged at his face. She had previously tried to explain to Wally, in so many words and dirty looks, that he was not and could not become an honorary black man through his love of Master P. He wore a vague smile that Fatima sometimes read as smug and sometimes as vapid, but he never seemed to hear her. He who would not hear, 35 however, would feel – or would have if Mrs. Bishop hadn't sent Fatima to the principal to 'cool down' before her fingernails could scratch off any of Wally's freckles.

It wasn't fair, Fatima thought, that Wally was praised, even mildly popular, for his FUBU shirts and Jordans with the tags still on them, yet 40 Fatima was called 'ghetto superstar' the one time she outlined her lips with dark pencil. Nor was it fair that she should get a warning from Principal Lee for 'looking like she might become violent' when Wally said 'nigger' and got applause. She was still thinking about Wally when she first encountered Violet.

45 They met at the Montclair Plaza, where Fatima had been dropped off by her mother, Monica, along with the warnings that she better not (1) exceed her allowance of fifty dollars; (2) use her emergency credit card for nonemergencies; or (3) pick up any riffraff, roughnecks, or pregnancies while she was there. Number three was highly unlikely, 50 and Fatima knew Monica knew it, but she said it anyway.

Fatima moped near the Clinique counter with her heavy Discman tucked in a tiny backpack and her headphones wrapped around her neck, trying to decide between one shade of lipstick and another. The college student behind the counter ignored her, chatting with another 55 colleague, and in situations like this, Fatima usually bought something expensive just to show the salesperson that she could. A blond girl with a short bob sauntered up next to her and said, 'The burgundy is pretty, but you could do something darker.'

Fatima peripherally saw the hair first, so she didn't expect the rest 60 of the package. A voluptuous – really, that was the only word that would work – girl with a wide nose and black features stood next to her. Fatima had a friend with albinism before in preschool who wore thick red glasses and had blushed almost the same color when she wet her pants at naptime once. She recognized in Violet similar features.

65 'But you could get the same stuff at Claire's for cheaper,' Violet said. 'It's not like old girl's trying to help you anyway.'

The salesgirl, not chastened but amused, moved back to her post and said, 'May I help you,' in one of those voices that mean 'Get lost.'

'I'm still –' Fatima started.

27 wrath [rɒθ]: anger
29 No Limit rapper: rapper who publishes music under No Limit Records, which belongs to Master P (born 1967), a US rapper and producer
33 smug [smʌg]: feeling very pleased about oneself
34 vapid ['væpɪd]: empty
39 FUBU = For us, by Us: US hip hop clothing company
39 Jordans: line of Nike trainers designed by Michael Jordan (born 1963), a former US professional basketball player
47 exceed sth.: go beyond what is expected
47 allowance: pocket money
48 riffraff ['rɪfræf] (derog): undesirable, lower class people
48 roughneck: sb. doing hard manual labour
51 Clinique [klɪ'niːk]: brand of make-up
57 burgundy: dark red
59 peripherally [pə'rɪfərəli]: just at the edge
60 voluptuous [və'lʌptʃuəs]: curvy
67 chastened ['tʃeɪsnd]: (here) embarrassed, sorry

70 But the blond black girl spoke again: 'We'd like some free samples of some of the lipsticks, that color'– she pointed, reaching over Fatima to a pot of dark gloss – 'and that one.'

'We only give samples,' the salesgirl said, 'to –'

'To everyone who asks, right?' Violet finished.

75 The sales associate frowned, looked back at her colleague, looked at Violet and Fatima, and frowned again. 'I'll get those ready for you,' she said.

Fatima considered putting her headphones back on and trying to float out of the department store, away from this loud girl with the
80 jarring features and booming voice.

'Here,' Violet said, handing her the dark gloss in its tiny gloss pot.

'You keep it,' Fatima said and started trying to vaporize toward the shoe department.

'It's for you,' the girl said, following her.

85 And like that, they were friends, or something to that effect.

* * *

It was Violet's appraisal – 'You're, like, totally a white girl, aren't you?' – that set Fatima into motion. They were eating dots of ice cream that same day at the food court after Violet showed Fatima how to get samples from Estée Lauder, Elizabeth Arden, and MAC. Fatima felt a
90 little like a gangster, holding up the reluctant salesgirls for their stash, but she had a nearly full bag of swag by then, perfume, lip gloss, and oil-blotting papers, without spending any of her allowance. It was already too good to be true, so she didn't feel sad when Violet said 'white girl,' but almost relieved by the inevitable.

95 Fatima had been accused of whiteness and being a traitor to the race before, whenever she spoke up in Sunday school at her AME church or visited her family in Southeast San Diego (Southeast a universal geographical marker for the ghetto) or when a cute guy who was just about to ask her out backed away, saying, 'You go to private school,
100 don't you?' It was why she didn't have any black friends – and why, she worried, she would never have a boyfriend, even riffraff to upset her mother.

The allegations offended her but never moved her to any action other than private crying or retreating further into her melancholy belief that
105 her school, Westwood Prep, and her parents' high-paying jobs, had made her somehow unfit for black people. Rather than respond, she usually turned up her Discman louder, sinking into the distantly black but presently white sounds of ska and punk, and sang under her breath, 'I'm a freak / I'm a freak' (in the style of Silverchair, not Rick James).
110 At the moment she especially enjoyed reading Charles Brockden Brown and daydreaming of a sickly boyfriend like Arthur Mervyn. If black people wouldn't accept her, she would stick to what she knew.

79 float (v): swim effortlessly
80 jarring [dʒɑːɹɪŋ]: unpleasant, too shrill
86 appraisal [əˈpreɪzl]: judgement
90 stash (n): (here) load of samples
91 swag [swæg]: (here) *Beute*
96 AME church: African Methodist Episcopal Church
103 allegation: accusation
109 Silverchair: Australian rock band
109 Rick James (1948–2004): African American singer-songwriter
110 Charles Brockden Brown [bɹɑkdən] (1771–1810): white US novelist
111 Arthur Mervyn [mɹvɪn]: character from a Charles Brockden Brown novel of the same name

But Violet's judgement held more heft, in her critique a possibility for transformation. When a black girl with natural green eyes and blond
115 hair and a big chest and bubble butt tells you that you, with your sable skin and dark hair, are not black enough, you listen.

'It's not that I'm trying to be white. It's just that it's what I'm around.'

'You don't have no church friends? You adopted? Your parents white, too?' Violet didn't seem to want a response. 'Where do you stay?'
120 'With my parents.' Fatima wondered if something was wrong with Violet for asking such a stupid question.

'I mean where do you live?' Violet asked.

'Upland.'

'They got black people there. My cousin Frankie lives there,' Violet
125 said, chewing the dots of ice cream in a way that set Fatima's teeth on edge. She wore a tight white top, cream Dickies, and white Adidas tennis shoes.

'Yes, but not on my street.' Fatima wore a pink cardigan, black Dickies, and skater shoes, Kastels.
130 Violet paused her crunching and talking for a moment. 'You have a boyfriend?'

Fatima shook her head. 'Do you?'

'I'm in between options right now. Anyway, the last one is locked up in Tehachapi.'
135 Fatima nodded. She had a cousin who had served time there. He called her bourgie, and she'd kicked him in the face once, delighting in his fat lip and his inability to hit girls.

'I'm kidding,' Violet said. 'We don't all get locked up.'

Fatima stuttered.
140 'I can see I'ma have to teach you a lot of things. You ready?' Violet meant ready to leave the food court, but Fatima meant more when she said, 'Yeah, I'm ready.' And thus began her transformation.

* * *

If only Baratunde Thurston had been writing when Fatima came of age, she could have learned how to be black from a book instead of from
145 Violet's charm school. Even a quick glance at Ralph Ellison could have saved her a lot of trouble, but she wasn't ready for that, caught up, as she was, in the dramas of Arthur Mervyn and Carwin, the Biloquist, and all of them. With Violet's help, Fatima absorbed the sociocultural knowledge she'd missed – not through osmosis or through more relevant
150 literature, but through committed, structured ethnographical study.

She immersed herself in slang as rigorously as she would later immerse herself in Spanish for her foreign-language exam in grad school; she pored over *Vibe* magazine and watched *Yo! MTV Raps* and *The Parkers*, trying to work her mouth around phrases with the same
155 intonation that Countess Vaughn used, a sort of combination of a Jersey

113 hold more heft: be more important
115 sable ['seɪbl]: *Zobel* (here) referring to the animal's black fur
126 Dickies (pl): brand of workwear
134 Tehachapi [tˈɛhætʃˌapi]: state prison in California
136 bourgie [bˈɜːdʒi] = bourgeois, belonging to the middle class, here used to criticize
143 Baratunde Thurston [bɑɹətʌnd θˈɜːstən] (born 1977): African American writer and comedian
145 Ralph Ellison (1914–1994): African American author
147 *Arthur Mervyn, Memoirs of Carwin the Biloquist*: novels by Charles Brockden Brown
150 committed: very determined
151 immerse sb./sth. in sth. [ɪˈmɜːs]: *eintauchen in etw.*
151 rigorously [ˈrɪɡərəsli]: carefully
153 *VIBE*: magazine for hip hop culture
154 *The Parkers*: US sitcom about a Black mother and daughter
155 Countess Vaughn [vˈɔːn] (born 1978): African American actress

26

accent and a speech impediment. When she couldn't get into those texts, she encouraged herself with the old episodes of *Fresh Prince of Bel-Air* that played in constant early-morning and late-night rotation, feeling assured that if Ashley Banks could, after five seasons, become almost
160 as cool as Will, then she could, too. Her new turns of phrase fit her about as awkwardly as the puffy powder-blue FUBU jacket she found in a thrift store in downtown Rialto.

Still, she was happy when Violet looked approvingly at it. Pale Violet became the arbiter of Fatima's blackness, the purveyor of all things
165 authentic. Though she was five feet eight and chunky by most standards – nearly obese by Fatima's – you would think Violet, judging by the way she walked, was Pamela Anderson, like a hula doll on a dashboard swinging hips and breasts.

The distance between their respective houses was fifteen minutes,
170 but only seven if they met halfway, Fatima borrowing her father's extra car (the 1993 Beamer, so as not to look ostentatious) and Violet getting a ride from one of her brothers or occasionally driving her mother's old Taurus. They never met at each other's houses, lest Fatima's upper-middle opulence embarrass Violet, and because there was no space for
175 Violet to carve out for herself at her house.

Violet made Fatima a study guide of the top ten black expressions for rating attractive men, and they practiced the pronunciations together. The pinnacle of hotness, according to Violet, was either 'dangfoine,' 'helly foine,' or 'bout it, bout it,' as in 'Oooh, he bout it, bout it.' This
180 phrase especially required the Countess Vaughn intonation and often included spontaneous bouts of raising the roof.

During their tutoring sessions, Fatima stifled her joke about the rain in Spain falling mostly on the plains and practiced on, assured that Violet's instruction would confer upon her, like Carwin, 'a wonderful
185 gift' of biloquism.

Glossaries soon followed, in which Violet broke down slang that had previously mystified Fatima. She couldn't wait to replace her traditional 'fer shure' with 'fisshow' in a real conversation, but she took issue with some of Violet's recommendations, especially 'nigga' and 'gangsta,'
190 which Violet explained as terms of endearment. 'So basically,' Fatima summarized, ventriloquizing Ashley Banks again, 'you want me to turn good things into bad things and vice versa.'

Violet said, 'Mostly.'

Fatima tried pumping her shoulders in a brief Bankhead Bounce, but
195 it was obvious she lacked the follow-through and wasn't ready for dancing yet.

And it was almost like any romantic comedy in which the sassy black person moves in with the white people and teaches them how to live their lives in color and put some bass in their voices, only Steve Martin
200 wasn't in it, and no one was a maid or a butler or nanny, and the romance

---

156 speech impediment [ɪmˈpedɪmənt]: physical problem with speaking
157 *Fresh Prince of Bel-Air*: US sitcom about a Black working-class teenager living with upper class family
159 Ashley/Will Banks: characters from the series *Fresh Prince of Bel-Air*
162 thrift store [ˈθrɪft] (AE) = charity shop (BE)
164 arbiter [ˈɑːbɪtə(r)]: mediator
164 purveyor [pəˈveɪə(r)]: supplier
165 chunky: fat
166 obese [əʊˈbiːs]: clinically overweight
167 Pamela Anderson (born 1967): US-Canadian actress and model
171 Beamer: Mercedes Benz
171 ostentatious [ˌɒstenˈteɪʃəs]: *protzig*
173 Taurus [tɔːrəs]: car model from Ford
174 opulence [ˈɒpjələns]: wealth
175 carve sth. out: (here) create sth.
178 pinnacle [ˈpɪnəkl]: optimum
181 raise the roof: be very noisy and lively
182 the rain in Spain: allusion to the musical *My Fair Lady*, in which a girl with a Cockney accent is taught to speak like a woman of higher class using this sentence
188 take issue with sb./ sth.: feel uncomfortable with sb./sth.
190 term of endearment [ɪnˈdɪəmənt]: *Kosewort*
192 vice versa [ˌvaɪs ˈvɜːsə]: the other way around
194 Bankhead Bounce: hip hop dance style
197 sassy [ˈsæsi] (infml, AE): (here) confident
199 Steve Martin (born 1945): US comedian and actor

was between two girls, and it was platonic, and they were both black this time, but one didn't look like it, and one didn't sound like it, at least not consistently.

* * *

'They racist up at that school?' I can't stand cocky white people,' Violet
205 said one day while they sat at their usual table, near the flower divider in the mall's arboretum. Some white guys from Hillwood sat across the way, laughing loudly.

Fatima didn't like to talk about her school, but everyone in the Inland Empire knew Westwood and Hillwood, rivals on and off the football
210 field. 'I don't think so,' Fatima said.

'What do you mean you don't think so? Either something's racist or it's not.'

No one at school poked out his tongue and called her *that*, like they did in the poem Wally read, but Fatima thought about Wally, his
215 affectations, and Principal Lee.

'It's not always comfortable,' she said. 'It can be awkward, but I'm awkward.'

'You sure are.' Violet laughed, and Fatima laughed, too. She was learning to do more of that, and to wear a kind of self-assuredness with
220 her side-swooped Aaliyah bangs.

In fact, most interactions were easier with Violet than they were with others. Violet understood things. Fatima never had to explain why she might wrap her hair in a silk scarf at bedtime or why she always carried a tube of hand cream to prevent not only chapped hands, but also allover
225 ashiness. Those shared practices validated Fatima, and so did Violet's understanding of Fatima's fears about her body. 'Sometimes I just feel horrible about all of it, the sweating, the bleeding. I don't always feel like a regular girl, you know?' Fatima said one day, 'But what is normal anyway?'

'Word, that's deep,' Violet said, and explained that she, too, felt the
230 weight of her body, because it did not look 'like what people expect black to be.' In spite of her seeming confidence, Violet confided, she had a complex about her albinism. Fatima understood when Violet intimated that albinism marked her as both desirable for her lightness, her hair color, her eye color, and yet despised for some perceived
235 physical untruth. Fatima had seen the way people glanced two or three times at Violet, deciding where to place her and whether she warranted any of the benefits of whiteness. Violet could call other black people like Fatima white, but to be called white herself pushed Violet to violent tears. Just ask her ex-boyfriend and her ex-friend Kandice from middle
240 school, who had called her Patti Mayonnaise in a fit of anger and gotten a beatdown that made her wet her pants like Fatima's preschool friend.

'Why Patti Mayonnaise?' Fatima said.

201 platonic: non-sexual
204 cocky ['kɒki] (infml): too full of oneself
206 arboretum [ˌɑːbəˈriːtəm]: small green space
220 Aaliyah [əlˈiːə] = Aaliyah Dana Haughton (1979–2001): US hip hop and R&B artist
220 bangs (pl): fringe
224 chapped [tʃæpt]: dry
225 validate sb./sth.: (here) give sense to sb./sth.
233 intimate sth. ['ɪntɪmeɪt]: hint at sth.
236 warrant sth.: make sth. necessary or fitting in a specific situation
240 Patti Mayonnaise: character from the cartoon series *Doug*

'You know, from *Doug*, she was the black girl on the DL who looked white, and mayonnaise is white. It's a stupid joke.'

245 'Patti was black?' Fatima said.

'Girl, a whole lot of everybody got black in them,' Violet started.

Fatima had heard some of Violet's theories before during a game they sometimes played on the phone. The list included Jennifer Beals, Mariah Carey, and 'that freaky girl from *Wild Things*,' Denise Richard,
250 and now, apparently, Patti Mayonnaise. When Fatima suggested Justin Timberlake, Violet said, 'Nah, he's like that Wally kid at your school.'

The nuances of these and other things Emily, Fatima's best friend since second grade, just couldn't understand, no matter how earnestly she tried or how many questions she asked, like why they couldn't share
255 shampoo when she slept over, or 'What does "For us, by us" even mean,' and why Fatima's top lip was darker than her bottom one.

Fatima picked up some theories on her own, too, without Violet or the literature. The thing about the brown top lip and the pink lower one, Fatima had pieced together after what she learned from Violet and
260 what she had learned at school, was that you could either read them as two souls trying to merge into a better self, or you could conceal them under makeup and talk with whichever lip was convenient for the occasion. At school and with Emily, she talked with her pink lip, and with Violet, she talked with her brown one, and that created tension
265 only if she thought too much about it.

* * *

Fatima passed the time at school by imagining the time she would spend after school with Violet, who promised to teach her how to flirt better on their next excursion and to possibly, eventually, hook her up with one of her cousins, but not one of her brothers, because 'Most of them
270 aren't good for anything except upsetting your mother, if you want to do that.' Fatima did not want to do that.

Now at school when Wally the Wigger looked like he was even thinking about saying something to her, Fatima made a face that warned, 'Don't even look like you're thinking about saying something
275 to me,' and he obeyed. In her mind, she not only said this aloud, but said it in Violet's voice.

She didn't mind the laughter in her parents' eyes when she tried out a new phrase or hairstyle, because it was all working. There was something prettier about her now too, and people seemed to see it
280 before Fatima did, because a guy named Rolf at Westwood – a tall brunette in her history class, with whom she'd exchanged a few eye rolls over Wally – asked her for her phone number.

Without pausing to consider anything, she gave it to him.

248 Jennifer Beals (born 1963): US actress
249 Mariah Carey (born 1969): US singer
249 *Wild Things*: US film from 1998
249 Denise Richards (born 1971): US singer
250 Justin Timberlake (born 1981): US singer
261 merge into sth.: unite sth.
261 conceal sb./sth.: hide sb./sth.
268 hook sb. up (with sb./sth.): (here) get sb. a date (with sb.)
281 brunette [bruːˈnet]: person with brown hair

29

It might seem, up to this point, that Fatima simultaneously wore braces,
285 glasses and forehead acne, when you hardly needed to glance to see
the gloss of her black hair or the sheen on her shins, with or without
lotion. Fatima knew this truth instinctively, but buried its warmth under
the shame of early-childhood teasing and preference for melancholy
self-pity. It was more romantic to feel ugly than to pretend she couldn't
290 hold her head just right, unleash her beautiful teeth, and make a
skeptical man kneel at her skirt's hem. She just didn't have the practice,
but she was hopeful that she might get it, with Rolf or one of Violet's
cousins, hopeful that the transformation had taken hold.

* * *

She had just returned from a movie with Violet – where not one but
295 two guys had asked for her phone number, though three had asked for
Violet's, pronouncing their approval of her 'thickness' with grunts,
smiles, and by looking directly at her butt – when her mother said, 'You
got a phone call, from a boy.'

It couldn't be one of the boys from the theater already; that would
300 make anyone look desperate.

'Who is Rolf?' her mother asked with a smile, 'and why didn't you
mention him before?'

Fatima nearly floated up to her bedroom. She thought about calling
Violet but called Rolf back instead, waiting, of course, for an hour to
305 pass, a tip she had learned from Violet in the event of a hypothetical
situation such as this.

By now, and with some authenticity, Fatima could intone the accent
marks in places they hadn't been before, recite all the names of the
members of Cash Money, Bada Boy, No Limit, Wu-Tang, Boyz II Men,
310 ABC, BBD, ODB, LDB, TLC, B-I-G-P-O-P-P-A, Ronny, Bobby, Ricky,
Mike, Ralph, Johnny, Tony, Toni and Tone, if she wanted. But when she
called Rolf, all they talked about were skateboards and The Smiths, in
whose music Fatima had dabbled before Violet.

'The Smiths are way better than Morrissey,' Rolf said. His voice was
315 nasal but deep.

'You can barely tell the difference since Morrissey's voice is so
overpowering,' she said, from her pink lip.

'No, but the Smiths' stuff is way darker,' Rolf said. 'You should hear
the first album. Then you'll get it. I've got it on vinyl.'
320 'Okay,' Fatima waited.

She noticed that he didn't invite her over to listen or offer to lend her
the album, but he did call back two days later and ask if she wanted to
hang out over the weekend, 'like at the mall or something, see a movie?'

Fatima counted to twelve, as per the rules (the universal ones, not
325 just Violet's) and said, 'Yeah, that'd be cool.' She almost left the 'l' off
the end of the word, but caught herself. 'Which mall?'

---

284 simultaneously [ˌsɪmlˈteɪniəsli]: at the same time
284 braces (AE): *Zahnspange*
286 sheen [ʃiːn] (n): shine
286 shin [ʃɪn]: *Schienbein*
288 preference [ˈprefrəns]: favourite choice
290 unleash sth.: let sth. have a strong effect
291 hem [hem]: lower line of a piece of clothing
293 take hold: be permanent
296 thickness: (here) fatness
296 grunt [grʌnt] (n): short low sound
297 butt: behind
303 float (v): (here) *schweben*
305 hypothetical [ˌhaɪpəˈθetɪkl]: speculative
307 intone sth.: *etw. betonen*
309 Cash Money, Bada Boy… Toni and Tone: hip hop artists
312 The Smiths: English rock band
313 dabble in sth. [ˈdæbl] (v): (hier) take a small interest in sth.
314 Morrissey = Steve Patrick Morrissey (born 1959): lead singer of the band The Smiths who also recorded solo albums
315 nasal: (here) sounding like a sound made through the nose

'Where else?' Rolf said. 'The Montclair Plaza.'

This would be her first date, and though that was the kind of thing to share with her best friend, especially the one with more experience,
330 Fatima felt – in some deep way that hurt her stomach – that Violet didn't need to know about Rolf, not yet at least. She would keep her lips glossed and parted, her two worlds separate.

* * *

The week leading up to the first date, Fatima tried to play extra-cool, asking Violet more questions than usual when they spoke on the phone.
335 Neither of the guys from the movie theater had called Fatima, but one of Violet's three had asked Violet out, and she was 'letting him stew for a little while before I let him know. Anyway, I thought you wanted to check out *Rush Hour* this weekend.'

'This weekend?' Fatima said.
340 'This weekend.'

'I told my parents I would babysit this weekend, I forgot.' Fatima lied, feeling a bit like a grease stain on a silk shirt.

'Since when?' Violet pushed.

'We can go next weekend, or during the week,' Fatima said, and
345 changed the subject.

Before they got off the phone, Violet said, 'I guess I'll call Mike back, then, and tell him I'm free after all.'

* * *

Fatima would say that she wasn't embarrassed by Violet or Rolf, but she wasn't ready for them to meet. She felt relief, then, when their first and
350 second dates went without a hitch – and ended with a gentle but sort of indifferent kiss – and even more relieved that Rolf was okay with seeing each other during the week so that Fatima wouldn't have to explain to Violet why she suddenly had other plans on Friday and Saturday evenings.

'Tell me more about your other friends,' Rolf said on the phone one
355 night, when Fatima was starting to think she might love him. He knew Emily from school. He knew she went to an AME church.

He'd met her parents and siblings by then, though she still hadn't met his. When he first came over to the house, he shook hands with Fatima's father – noting Mr. Willis's height with a 'Whoa, you're tall' – and hugged
360 her mother and patted her six-year-old brother's head awkwardly, in a way that reminded Fatima of someone stroking a rabbit's foot for luck.

At dinner Rolf chatted to excess, complimenting the drapes, the silverware, and Fatima's frowny-faced eight-year-old sister and indifferent younger brother. She wasn't sure how nervous either of
365 them should be. She found his foot with hers under the table and smiled silently, 'Calm down. Be quiet.' She tried to signal, but Rolf prattled on, 'I think it's great that you as a black family are so successful.'

336 stew [stjuː] (v): (here) wait or worry
338 *Rush Hour*: action film from 1998 starring US-Chinese actor Jackie Chan (born 1964) and US actor Chris Tucker (born 1971)
342 grease: fat
349 relief [rɪˈliːf]: *Erleichterung*
350 hitch [hɪtʃ]: problem
360 pat sb./sth. [pæt] (v): touch sb./sth. lightly several times
362 drape (AE): curtain
366 prattle [ˈprætl] (v, old-fashioned): talk nonstop about sth. unimportant

31

No one addressed Rolf, but her parents stood to clear the dishes. She heard their irritation in faint whispers from the kitchen, could see it in their eyes even with their backs turned. Fatima declined dessert. 'We have to get to the movies. We'll get some candy there,' she said.

Still, she and Rolf were together a month later, and her parents hadn't expressed any concrete disapproval. A month later, she was only just telling Rolf about Violet.

'I guess my other best friend,' Fatima responded, 'besides Emily, is Violet.'

'Violet,' Rolf repeated. 'Cool name. She's not at Westwood, is she?'

'No, public school.'

'Ah,' Rolf said, in a tone that Fatima interpreted as neutral.

'She's my girl.' She stopped herself from saying 'Ace boon coon.' 'We hang out a lot on the weekends, actually.'

'How come you never mentioned her before?'

'I don't know.' Fatima felt her mouth lying again, moving somehow separately from her real voice. 'She's kind of shy. She got teased a lot.'

'Oh that's too bad,' Rolf said.

'They called her Patti Mayonnaise,' Fatima said, and she didn't know why it was she who was now prattling on.

'Don't tell anybody this, but I always thought Patty was cute on Doug,' Rolf said, and shifted to talk about about all his favorite cartoons. Fatima exhaled.

* * *

Over time they grew to joke, a little awkwardly, about Fatima's position at school, as one of the two black girls. She asked Rolf if this was a thing for him or if she was his first black girlfriend, because by now they called each other boyfriend and girlfriend.

'I don't see color,' he said. 'I just saw you. Like, one day there you were.'

Violet would have said that color-blind people were the same ones who followed you in the store and that Rolf's game was hella corny.

'Anyway, it's not like you're black black,' Rolf said.

Fatima remembered the lifelessness, before Violet, of feeling like a colorless gas and tried, in spite of a dull ache and the numbness of her brown lip, to take Rolf's words as a compliment.

* * *

The conventions of such a transformation dictate that a snaggletooth or broken heel threatens to return the heroine to her former life. That snaggletooth, for Fatima, was either Rolf or Violet, depending on how you looked at things, and Fatima wasn't sure how she did.

When she saw Violet, on April 4 – after hiding her relationship with Rolf for three months – approaching from across the lobby of Edwards Cinema with Mike's arm around her waist, Fatima's first instinct was to

---

370 decline sth.: politely say no to sth.
380 coon (derog): offensive word for a Black person
390 exhale: let air out of your lungs
397 hella (infml): very
397 corny: sentimental, not original
400 dull [dʌl]: not sharp
402 snaggletooth [ˈsnægltuːθ] (infml): tooth that is noticeably different or strange

---

410 grab Rolf's hand and steer him toward the exit. But Violet was already calling her name.

This wasn't the natural order of things, for these separate lives to converge. Other factors aside, the code went hos before bros, school life before social life, family before anyone else. But Rolf was both school and social, and Violet both social and nearly family, and Fatima's math skills couldn't balance this equation.

415 'I knew I saw you,' Violet said to Fatima once she got close. 'Who is this?'

'Rolf, Violet. Violet, Rolf,' Fatima said, 'and Mike.'

Mike smiled, and Rolf smiled, and they shook hands, but neither young woman saw the guys, their eyes deadlocked on each other.

420 'Ha, so this is Violet,' Rolf said, ignoring or misreading Fatima's firm grip on his arm. 'Even your black friends are white, too.' Rolf laughed.

'I was gonna tell you –' Fatima started to say to Violet.

'Wait, Patti Mayonnaise, I get it now,' Rolf said aloud, then, 'Oops, I –' and both women scowled at him.

425 Fatima made a noise that could be interpreted as either a guffaw or a deep moan.

When she turned back to Violet, though she opened and closed her mouth several times, no sounds emerged. She didn't mean to hurt her; some things had just come out, and other things she hadn't told Violet 430 because she wasn't sure which lip she was supposed to use. Before she knew it, her voice was over there and then over there, and she was ventriloquizing what she'd learned all at once, but from too many places and all at the wrong time.

Violet didn't curse or buck up as though she might hit Fatima – 435 though perhaps one of those options might have been better; she just grabbed Mike's arm and walked away.

And like that, Fatima was vapor again, but something darker, like a funnel cloud, or black smoke that mocked what was already singed.

From: *Heads of the Colored People*, Vintage, 2019, pp. 65–81.

---

412 converge: come close
412 hos before bros (infml): *Luder vor Bruder*
419 deadlock on sb./sth.: (here) be fixed on sb./sth.
424 scowl at sb./sth. [skaʊl]: frown at sb./sth.
425 guffaw [gəˈfɔː]: noisy laugh
428 emerge [ɪˈmɜːdʒ]: come out
432 ventriloquize [venˈtrɪləkwaɪz]: *bauchreden*
434 buck up [bʌk ʌp] (infml): (here) brace up, become encouraged
438 funnel cloud [ˈfʌnl klaʊd]: *Trichterwolke*

Info Nafissa Thompson-Spires

Nafissa Thompson-Spires (born 1983) is an African American writer of fiction and non-fiction who has won several awards. She has a Master's Degree in Creative Writing and a doctorate in English Literature. In her writing she mainly concentrates on questions of Black identity, but also on mental health issues. She feels particularly inspired by Black writers. As an academic, Thompson-Spires also teaches literature, creative writing and television studies at Cornell University.

Comprehension

2 Read the following statements and tick whether they are true or false.
Support your answer with a quote and line number(s) from the text.

Statement	True	False
A At the start of the story Fatima is not a very self-confident girl.	○	○
Line(s): _____		
Quote: _____		
B Fatima likes the way her classmate Wally is interested in Black artists.	○	○
Line(s): _____		
Quote: _____		
C At their first meeting, Fatima is slightly overwhelmed by Violet and her self-confidence.	○	○
Line(s): _____		
Quote: _____		
D Violet's criticism makes Fatima want to change because she does not feel Black enough.	○	○
Line(s): _____		
Quote: _____		
E Violet makes Fatima study the literature of Black writers to become more Black.	○	○
Line(s): _____		
Quote: _____		
F Violet reacts strongly to being called 'Patti Mayonnaise'.	○	○
Line(s): _____		
Quote: _____		

Statement	True	False
G Violet feels that Fatima behaves differently according to the people she is with. Line(s): _____ Quote: _____	○	○
H People at her school don't seem to notice the change in Fatima. Line(s): _____ Quote: _____	○	○
I Fatima hurries to tell Violet about her first date with Rolf. Line(s): _____ Quote: _____	○	○
J Fatima's parents like Rolf. Line(s): _____ Quote: _____	○	○

3 Outline the change shown in Fatima.

Analysis

4 Draw a character map for the short story to show the relationships between the characters.

5 a Analyse the imagery used to describe Black people in the first paragraph.

  b Explain the simile (→ Info box) in the second paragraph.

> **Info Simile and metaphor**
> A simile ['sɪməli] is a comparison of two ideas marked by 'like' or 'as'. A metaphor ['metəfɔː(r)] is the linking of two ideas that are normally not linked without using 'like' or 'as'.

6 a Describe how Wally is characterized.

  b Explain why Fatima does not like the way he behaves.

7 **a** Do some further research on the music or the styles of clothing mentioned in the story.
 b Explain how these attributes are used to characterize Fatima and other characters.
8 Explain the following quote from the story:

> 'And like that, they were friends, or something to that effect.' (l. 85).

What does their friendship seem to be based on?

9 Contrast Violet and Fatima. According to Fatima's own idea of what it means to be Black, why does Violet seem more 'Black' than Fatima?
10 Examine the concepts of 'white' and 'Black' used in the story. Consider music, places, family, social aspects, etc. Is it possible to state that these concepts belong only to one racial group?
11 Analyse the metaphor (→ Info box, p. 35) of Fatima's two lips throughout the story.

Beyond the text

12 **a** Discuss whether you think Wally's behaviour is racist.
 b Explain why Fatima hesitates to reject the idea that the white people at her school are racist (ll. 204–217)?
13 Comment on the idea that Fatima wants to keep her two worlds apart.

14 Work on either **a**, **b**, or **c**.
 a **Writing** Write three of Fatima's diary entries (→ Info box, p. 87) for the following days:
  A her first meeting with Violet
  B one of her dates with Rolf
  C meeting Violet in the cinema
 b **Writing** Think about Rolf's behaviour at Fatima's parents' house. Write three different interior monologues (→ Info box) that express what each of the following characters could be thinking during the visit.
  A Rolf
  B Fatima
  C Fatima's parents
 c **Writing** Continue the story. What happens next?
15 In groups, discuss why it is offensive to state that someone is an 'oreo' or a 'wigger'. What does it reveal about people's ideas of ethnicity? Do you agree with this concept?

Info Interior monologue
An interior monologue is a type of scenic presentation in which a character's thoughts and feelings are depicted. When performing an interior monologue, put yourself in the character's shoes. 'Your' thoughts do not have to be in chronological order. It is common to present them as reported speech, using reporting verbs such as *think*. Use the first-person perspective.

B3 'Heads of the Colored People: Four Fancy Sketches, Two Chalk Outlines, and No Apology' *Nafissa Thompson-Spires*

1 Read the title of the short story and speculate what it could be about.
2 **a** Do some online research about the 'Say her name' campaign.
 b Share what you found with the class.

Read the short story 'Heads of the Colored People: Four Fancy Sketches, Two Chalk Outlines, and No Apology' by Nafissa Thompson-Spires and complete the tasks on pp. 45–46.

1.

Riley wore blue contact lenses and bleached his hair – which he worked with gel and a blow-dryer and a flatiron some mornings into Sonic the Hedgehog spikes so stiff you could prick your finger on them, and sometimes into a wispy side-swooped bob with long bangs – and he
5 was black. But this wasn't any kind of self-hatred thing. He's read *The Bluest Eye* and *Invisible Man* in school and even picked up *Disgruntled* at a book fair, and yes, they were good and there was some resonance in those books for him, but this story isn't about race or 'the shame of being alive' or any of those things. He was not self-hating; he was even

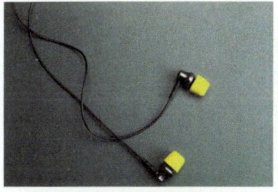

10 listening to Drake – though you could make it Fetty Wap if his appreciation for trap music changes something for you, because all that's relevant here is that he wasn't against the music of 'his people' or anything
15 like that – as he walked down Figueroa with his earbuds pushed in just far enough so as not to feel itchy.

Riley was wearing the wispy swooped version of his bangs and listening to Drake or Fetty, and he was black with blue contacts and bleached-blond hair. And yes, there are black people who have both of
20 those things naturally, without the use of artificial accouterments, so we can move past the whole phenotypically this or biologically that discussion to the meat of things. And if there is something meta in this narrator's consciousness and self-consciousness or this overindulgent aside, it isn't meta for the sake of being meta; this narrator's consciousness
25 is just letting you know about said consciousness up front, like a raised black fist, to get the close reading out of the way and make space for Riley, who was the kind of black man for whom blue eyes and blond hair were not natural. He was the kind of black that warranted – or invited without solicitation – comparisons to drinks from Starbucks or
30 lyrics from 'Lady Marmalade' or chocolate bars, with nuts.

00 fancy: elegant, smart
2 Sonic the Hedgehog: character from a videogame
4 wispy ['wɪspi]: thin
4 bangs (pl, AE) = fringe (BE)
5 *The Bluest Eye*: novel by Toni Morrison
6 *Invisible Man*: novel by Ralph Ellison
6 *Disgruntled*: novel by Asali Solomon
7 resonance: power to bring images to the mind of the reader
10 Drake (born 1986): Canadian rapper and hip hop artist
11 Fetty Wap (born 1991): US rapper and hip hop artist
15 Figueroa Street [fɪgɛɹowə]: major street in Los Angeles
16 itchy ['ɪtʃi]: *juckend*
20 accouterments [ə'kuːtrəmənts] (fml. pl): pieces of equipment
21 phenotypically [fɪnətɪpɪkli]: characterized by a set of observable genetics
23 overindulgent [ˌəʊvərɪn'dʌldʒent]: (here) very elaborate
28 warrant sth. ['wɒrənt]: guarantee sth.
29 solicitation [səˌlɪsɪ'teɪʃn]: formal request

You would think with his blue contacts and unnaturally blond hair set against dark chocolate mocha-choca-latte-yaya skin – and yes, there is some judgement in the use of 'you' – that Riley would date white or Asian women exclusively, or perhaps that he liked men. But you'd be

35 wrong on all counts, as Riley was straight, and he dated widely among black women, and he was neither in denial, nor on the down-low, nor, like John Mayer, equal opportunity and United Colors of Benetton in life but as separate as the fingers of the hand in sex, nor like Frederick Douglass or many others working on black rights in public and going

40 home to a white wife (and there is no judgement against Douglass here, just facts for the sake of descriptive clarity). Riley liked black women, both their blackness and womanness and the overlap between those constructs; nor was Riley queerphobic or the type of man to utter 'no homo' in uncomfortable situations, because Riley was comfortable

45 enough, if 'enough' expresses a sort of educated awareness. There is so much awareness in these two paragraphs that I have hardly made space for Riley, who in addition to black women liked cosplay – dressing up as characters from his favorite books and movies – and *Dr. Who* and *Rurouni Kenshin* and the Comic-Love convention, and especially *Death*

50 *Note*, his favorite manga and anime series. And though that day he was dressed as Tamaki Suoh (per his girlfriend's request), in a skinny periwinkle suit with a skinny black tie, his appearance gave him the flexibility to on other occasions dress as Kise Ryouta or Naruto, or, if he was feeling especially bold, Super Saiyan.

55 So it was bothersome, then, to Riley/Tamaki as he walked toward the Los Angeles Convention Center, when Brother Man at the corner of Figueroa and Fifteenth – not to be confused with the Original Bruh Man, whose actual origins or current whereabouts are unknown, but Bruh Man's gradated type, this particular yet stock Bruh Man, Brother Man –

60 accosted Riley after he brushed away the pamphlet Brother Man was trying to hand him and put his hand on Riley's shoulder and ventured to violate Riley's personal space even further by using that large hand with cigarette-stained fingernails to turn Riley toward him. I am saying Brother Man stopped Riley on the street, singled him out in front of

65 people dressed, respectively, as Princess Mononoke, Storm, Daleks, Cybermen, and Neil deGrasse Tyson (both in blackface and in their own black faces), put his hands on him, and forced him to look into Brother Man's own face with the familiarity of a friend yet, contextually, with the violence of a stranger.

70 On any other day Riley might have acknowledged that he was wrong to walk past Brother Man's initial 'Howyoudoin,' which he pretended not to hear on account of the Fetty. On this day, however, Riley felt that since he was inhabiting the character of Tamaki, his decision to ignore Brother Man was just right, an exercise in method acting.

36 on the down low: in secret
37 John Mayer (born 1977): US musician and singer
38 Frederick Douglass (1818–1895): African American social reformer, abolitionist and writer
43 no homo (infml): phrase that signals that a statement has no homosexual double meaning
48 *Dr. Who*: British science fiction series
49 *Rurouni Kenshin*: Japanese manga series
51 Tamaki Suoh: anime character from the anime and manga series *Ouran High School Host Club*
52 periwinkle ['periwɪŋkl]: *Immergrün*
53 Kise Ryouta, Naruto, Super Saiyan: manga characters
58 Bruh [bɹʌ] (infml): brother
58 Bruh Man: character in the US TV series *Martin*
60 accost sb. [əˈkɒst]: speak to sb. very persistently
65 Princess Mononoke, Storm … Tyson: cosplay costumes of fantasy and manga characters
66 blackface: use of makeup to appear Black

75   Riley was more than surprised – and did not need to borrow Tamaki's affectations to feel slighted – that Brother Man had touched him, and by that point, even though he might have been just the kind of buyer for what Brother Man was selling, his pride wouldn't let him concede.

* * *

It had long irked Riley that his blackness or the degree of his loyalty to
80 the cause should be suspect because he wore blue contacts and bleached his hair blond and because, on top of all that, his name was also Riley, and not, say, Ryreke. It irked him that he might be mistaken for a self-hating Uncle Tom because he enjoyed cosplay and anime and comic book conventions and because he happened to be feeling the character
85 of a rich Japanese schoolboy a little too much at that very moment.

   By the time Brother Man said, 'Uppity, gay-looking nigga,' Riley had bypassed logic and forgotten that he held none of the privileges of his costume.

   There ensued then what Riley, in his costume, might have called
90 fisticuffs, though in everyday life he would have simply said they got to scrappin, right on Figueroa Street.

   The people who watched and filmed and circulated the scene from inside one of the lobbies of the convention center said it was just like Naruto v. Pain, only with two black guys, so you couldn't tell if either
95 one was the hero.

2.

In truth, Brother Man was burly but not violent and rather liked to regard himself as an intellectual in a misleading package. If he could have made a wish before the end of the day, it would have been that he, too, had worn a costume to soften the effects of his image.
100   When he put his hand on Riley's shoulder, it was only because he disliked the sight of someone, especially one of his own, turning his back to him without hearing him out. It was also because he needed to promote *Brother's Spawn* and had thus far convinced a meager four passersby to buy a $4 copy that day, and because Brother Man felt,
105 unapologetically, that black people should stick together and that the blue-eyed, wig-wearing brother in the purple suit should have at least acknowledged him with a nod, if not a handshake or a howyoudoin.

   Though in the aftermath, people would call his papers religious tracts, indoctrination materials, and 'some kind of gang documents', *Brother*
110 *Spawn* was Brother Man's self-published dystopic comic series set at Pasadena City College, where he first learned of Octavia Butler and her work. The comics were hand-drawn with the dimensions of a postcard, though he also hoped to sell broadsides featuring a poem he had written.

   Brother Man – aliases Kyle Barker, Cole Brown, Overton Wakefield
115 Jones, Tammy Strawn, and pen name Brother Hotep – was selling the

76 slighted: treated without respect
78 concede sth.: admit that sth. is true after denying it
79 irk sb. [ɜːk]: annoy sb.
83 Uncle Tom: main character of Harriet Beecher Stowe's novel *Uncle Tom's Cabin*; often used to negatively describe a Black person acting too compliant around white people
86 uppity [ˈʌpəti]: arrogant
89 ensue: follow
90 fisticuffs [ˈfɪstɪkʌfs] (pl, old-fashioned): fist fight
96 burly [ˈbɜːli]: big, strong and heavy
103 meager: not enough
111 Octavia Butler (1947–2006): African American science fiction author
113 broadside: *Einblattdruck*
115 pen name: fake name used by a writer instead of their real name

Downtown Los Angeles

postcard comics illegally (he preferred the term 'without official city permits') between a food truck and a juice cart that day. On other days he sold them near the Century City Mall, in Ladera Heights, in Little Ethiopia, and as far as Inglewood.

120   That day, he banked on the convention center's Comic-Love traffic and the potential readers it might attract, boasting to his girlfriend earlier in the morning that he would probably sell out, 'even without one of those official tables in the convention center, watch.'

    And though he would say he was not usually the type to call Riley
125 a sellout or an Uncle Tom, that day, Brother Man (real name Richard Simmons, yes, Richard Simmons) could not handle Riley's refusal to acknowledge him or his art. He could find reasons to dismiss the hundred or so people in costumes, some speaking English, some other languages, who shook their hands no at the laminated mock-ups he tried to show
130 them, but he could not abide a black refusal, especially one from a black guy in a Japanese prep-schoolboy costume, the very kind of audience Brother Man hoped to cultivate.

    Thus, when he put his hand on Riley's shoulder, he never meant to hit him, and if he could, Brother Man, hereafter Richard, would have
135 imagined that Riley didn't plan to fight him either. And neither man ever would have thought that amateur karate (pronounce in the authentic Japanese accent) would be involved, their arms flailing and legs kicking out in poorly choreographed mortal combat.

3.

On his way to a meeting, Kevan stopped at the SweetArt Bakeshop in
140 Saint Louis to purchase a vegan brownie for himself and a purple cupcake with tiny candy hearts for his daughter Penny, who was with him for the weekend. The whole shop was lined with canvases of varying sizes, painted by the owners and sold from the bakery, which served as a gallery and community meeting space. Tiny vases holding local flowers
145 adorned each table. Kevan wore a black T-shirt that said in white letters, 'Eff Your Respectability Politics.' He liked the irony of the word 'eff' instead of the F-word, but he still debated whether it was better to change 'your' to 'yo'. He wasn't sure if anyone understood the stakes in these decisions or in any of his other art, which he sold online, from
150 his car, and occasionally from a small suitcase in the barbershop on Washington Avenue.

    He had one hour left with Penny before her mother would pick her up so Kevan could meet a potential business partner and pitch an idea he couldn't shake.

155   He chose a table in the middle of the nearly empty shop, with yellow-and-green flowers in the vase. 'She's a superhero,' Penny said, pointing to the largest canvas on the wall adjacent to the bakery case, and inhaling another glob of frosting. The frosting accumulated at the

125 sellout (infml): (here) traitor
127 dismiss sb./sth.: wave sb./sth. aside because you feel they are/it is unimportant
129 mock-up ['mɒk ʌp] (n): model
132 cultivate sb./sth.: (here) attract sb./sth.
137 flail: move around uncontrolledly
142 canvas ['kænvəs]: (here) painting
145 adorn sb./sth. [əˈdɔːn]: decorate sb./sth.
148 stake in sth.: risk of sth.
153 pitch sth. [pɪtʃ] (v): (here) present, introduce sth.
157 adjacent to sth. [əˈdʒeɪsnt]: next to sth.
158 glob [glɒb] (infml): *Klumpen*
158 frosting (AE) = icing (BE): *Glasur*
158 accumulate: (here) increase slowly

corners of Penny's smile, but her tongue missed those spots each time
160 it swept her mouth.

'She's cute. Daddy can teach you to paint like this,' Kevan said, passing Penny a napkin across the table.

Kevan wasn't a vegan, but he supported black business and black art, and regarded SweetArt as a place where his own work might one
165 day be presented. The T-shirt sales provided him a stash of petty cash, but Kevan had sold only three paintings, and that grieved him. He supported his daughter Penny with a court order and a 'real job' as a UPS deliveryman, but he 'always took care of my responsibilities,' even before Penny's mother, whom he alternately called a gold digger, that
170 whore, and my queen, demanded official monthly payments.

'My superhero name is gonna be –' Penny paused to pull back the wrapper and expose the last quarter of the cupcake, its frosting smooshed and all the candy hearts gone –'my name's gonna be Purple. Purple Penny Powers. I will make things purple like this,' Penny said, zapping
175 something with her arm.

'Purple Penny Powers.' Kevan pretended this was cuter than it was. 'Wow'.

He was trying not to think about a joke he had seen earlier in the day, trying not to remember the sight of the two dead bodies that had
180 appeared casually in his news feed, trying to rehearse instead his pitch for the realization of something he had read in a book that he found in a used bookstore.

The Afric-American Picture Gallery was a series of written sketches by William Wilson, under the pen name Ethiop and following the form
185 of similar sketches — which Kevan found with more research — by James McCune Smith in *The Heads of the Colored People* and Jane Rustic (a.k.a. Frances Ellen Watkins Harper, a black abolitionist poet and suffragist). Kevan wanted to commission painters, including mostly himself, to create a full exhibit of heads of the colored people, now and
190 then, to take the written, literary work and render it visually. The idea intrigued him, the heads talking to him like the books in Equiano – though he didn't know that reference yet.

In Kevan's collection, there would be, as in Ethiop's original, Phyllis Wheatley, Nat Turner, and a doctor, but he would update his favorite
195 sketch, 'Picture 26,' of the 'colored youth' who was 'surrounded by abject wretchedness' to reflect a sort of current abjection. To these he would add a superhero for Penny and a collage for the black men (and women, he would concede, with some coaxing later from Paris Larkin) who had been killed by police and other brutalities.
200 'Now what's your name going to be?' Penny's voice seemed especially shrill at the moment.

'I don't know.' Kevan was still thinking about the bodies and the grainy video of the two men arguing and the way one of the men had held out

---

165 petty cash [ˌpeti ˈkæʃ]: small amount of money
166 grieve sb. [griːv]: (here) make sb. sad
167 court order: *gerichtliche Mahnung*
169 gold digger (infml, derog): person only interested in using other people for money
170 whore [hɔː(r)] (derog): woman who works as a prostitute
172 smooshed: *zerquetscht*
188 commission sb. to do sth.: *jdm. etw. in Auftrag geben*
190 render sth.: (here) show sth.
191 Olaudah Equiano [əˈlaʊdə ɛkwɒɑnoʊ] (1745–1797): African American ex-slave who became a writer and abolitionist
193 Phyllis Wheatley (1753–1784): first African American author who published poetry
194 Nat Turner (1800–1831): enslaved African American preacher who led a slave rebellion in 1831
196 abject [ˈæbdʒekt] (adj, fml): terrible, without hope
196 wretchedness [ˈretʃɪdnəs]: unhappiness
196 abjection: state of sadness
202 grainy: not very clear

his hand when the police officer entered the scene; it was clear that the
205 man wasn't holding a gun or a knife, but something soft, like paper.

'Daddy, your name,' Penny demanded.

'I don't know,' Kevan repeated and blurted out the first thing that
came to mind: 'Bruh Man.'

'Bruh Man?' Penny jutted her head back. 'What does he do?'

210 'He paints, and whatever he wishes, he can paint it and make it
happen.' Kevan made Penny lick a napkin so he could wipe the leftover
icing from her face. 'And he can make bad things unhappen, if he paints
them right.'

'That's gonna be my power, too,' Penny said, pulling away from his
215 grooming and hesitating in the way of five-year-olds, 'but I'm just gonna
think and make it happen or unhappen.'

4.

Paris Larkin was meeting Riley at the convention center after two shifts
at her part-time job for Dark Shadows Hollywood Cemetery Tours. Her
official job description said, 'Tour Narrator: Vocal Talent. Must be able
220 to memorize stories and stand for long periods of time on moving bus
while engaging audiences.' I ain't saying she a gravedigger, Riley liked
to begin when he introduced her as his girlfriend, but really, she digs
graves, like, loves them. It was one of the things that had attracted him
to her when they first met, her dark cheeriness and her nonjudgemental
225 approach to his lifestyle. And his soft-landing punch lines were one of
the things Paris liked about him, and his interesting face, and the way
he wasn't at all who she expected him to be.

When he took his contact lenses out at night and tied his hair down
 with a durag, Riley looked just as comfortable and kind as when
230 he dressed up and hung out at his favorite comic café in
Pasadena, drinking boba tea and playing chess with kids from
Caltech, where he studied engineering and was one of a
handful of black students on campus.

If Paris could have a superpower, it would be to make herself visible,
235 because even though she stood at the front of the bus with a
microphone, pointing out alleged sightings of Marilyn Monroe to
hungry tourists with camera phones and Gucci sunglasses, she wasn't
the main attraction, and she preferred to narrate the tours with
reverence instead of theatrics, to fade into the background and let the
240 spirits speak for themselves. With Riley she could be seen, since they
got a decent amount of attention when they were together and
especially when they dressed up. Certain cosplay purists (read: racists)
did not always approve of Paris's or Riley's respective costume choices
or the idea of black people dressed as nonblack characters. Paris had
245 come to anticipate and almost enjoy the surge of anxiety that came
with entering these spaces, had felt her flight-or-fight instinct the

215 grooming: process of keeping yourself clean and presentable
225 punch line: climax of a joke
229 durag [duːræg]: head scarf that is tied behind the head
231 boba tea: bubble tea
232 Caltech: California Institute of Technology
236 alleged [əˈledʒd]: *angeblich*
239 reverence [ˈrevərəns]: feeling of admiration and respect
239 theatrics (pl): a lot of playacting
241 decent: (here) good enough
245 surge of sth. [sɜːdʒ]: sudden increase of sth.

closest thing to being fully alive. And the ghost tours, too, made her think that by comparison, she was at least more alive than the bodies that filled those holes.

250   That day was not her day off, so she took the Metro and two buses to meet Riley at the convention after work, after showering and changing into her long silver wig and meticulously sewn necromancer dress, her dark skin contrasting with the purple-and-white pinstripes of the dress, the gray armor on her arms and legs elevating her mood. She had
255 debated dressing as Haruhi Fujioka, the counterpart to Riley's costume from *Ouran High School Host Club*, but her choice of Eucliwood Hellscythe created a bigger impact, she thought. Though she kept her blue contacts down and focused on her sketchbook, her eyelids, adorned with heavy black-and-white shadow, warned other transit passengers
260 to dare her, that day.

  When Paris entertained visitors from out of town, or when she and Riley caught the spirit, she liked to ride the Metrolink from Highland Park to Glendale to visit Michael Jackson's mausoleum, which you couldn't exactly get close to, but which still sent a melancholy shiver
265 through her and her guests. During most of her time on the bus or the Metrolink, Paris drew Riley and many other people — you could call her a sketch artist, though not in any official, paying capacity.

  She called her sketchbooks a collection of heads, for she never drew bodies, and anyway, Paris was lighthearted and laughed frequently,
270 showing the gap between her teeth, not nearly as morbid as her job and curated heads made her sound. She called Riley Fuzzy Lumpkins, and he called her Bubbles. She was listening to 'Say My Name,' attached as she was to all things nineties, even though she was nineteen and had been born after Tupac or Biggie were already dead. That morning, Paris
275 had watched rerurns of *Martin* and laughed at a character's plea for a wish sandwich. In the nineties, she felt — and you should fill in for yourself a kind of longing here — something melancholy, plaid, flannel, but not overwrought.

  It isn't true, at least not in Paris's case, that you can sense what the
280 future holds. That day, she had jokingly, in an exercise of character acting, avoided pronouncing Riley's name near the word 'death' or at the graveyard or while dressed as Eucliwood, lest she kill him. But no psychic, metaphysical force warned her to tell Riley not to go to Comic-Love or to avoid arguments without spoils or to immediately put his
285 hands up when instructed to do so. Nothing told her, still humming 'Say My Name' in her best humming voice, not to walk toward the large crowd of flashing lights, police cars, and costumed and uncostumed bystanders. Her stomach urged her to look away, once she got close enough to be sickened, but she couldn't then.

290   She didn't feel more alive from the surge of panic in her body or in comparison to Riley on the ground.

252 meticulously: with great attention to detail
252 necromancer: *Geisterbeschwörerin*
253 pinstraip ['pɪnstraɪp]: *Nadelstreifen*
254 armor ['ɑːmə(r)]: *Rüstung*
254 elevate sth.: lift sth. up
256 Eucliwood Hellscythe [uːkliwʊd helsaɪð]: fictional character from the novel/anime series *Is This a Zombie* who raises zombies
264 shiver ['ʃɪvə(r)] (n): *Frösteln*
270 morbid ['mɔːbɪd]: interested in death
271 curated: put in an exhibition
274 Tupac Shakur [ˌtuːpæk ʃəˈkʊə(r)] (1971–1996): US rapper and hip hop artist
274 Biggie ['bɪgi] = Christopher George Latore Wallace (1972–1997): also known as the Notorious B.I.G or Biggie Smalls, US rapper and songwriter
275 rerun (n): *Reprise, Wiederholung*
275 *Martin*: US TV sitcom
275 plea [pliː]: emotional request
278 overwrought [ˌəʊvəˈrɔːt]: exhausted and excited
284 spoils (pl, fml): (here) winnings you get from being successful

Years later, she would regret not drawing the offending officer that
day. Since then, she has sketched his face over and over, penciling his
name and image in her notebook as a sort of plea, saying it aloud,
295 wishing that she, like Eucliwood, could pronounce the names of those
she wanted to die and make it so.

When an artist named Kevan Peterson wrote to her about a project
he wanted to finish — really, to finally begin — Paris was glad for her
sketches of Riley.

Woman with cornrows

5.

300 A well-read, self-aware, self-loving black man with blue contact lenses
and blond hair and a periwinkle suit was shot down in Los Angeles after
a reportedly violent altercation with a well-read street promoter, who
was also shot, after police officers answered a complaint. 'Who was also
shot' here signals the afterthought that was Brother Man, Richard,
305 because he was not the one with the blond hair or blue contacts or in
any way exceptional, except for his size and the things he had overcome
(too many to name here), and his comic books.

And you should fill in for yourself the details of that shooting as long
as the constants (unarmed men, excessive force, another dead body,
310 another dead body) are included in those details. Hum a few bars of 'Say
My Name', but in third person plural if that does something for you.

A few more points I should not leave to the imagination: in the chalk
drawing on Fifteenth, you can see Riley's leg kicking out like Spike
Spiegel and an additional rectangle above the outline of Richard's hand,
315 where he might have held his comic books or a laminated mock-up.

The picture the Associated Press chose from a Throwback Thursday
photo that Riley had posted on social media, a picture of him in a
costume from an undergrad party, at which he wore an oversize blue
shirt and a bedazzled blue bandana over cornrows. His mother, and
320 girlfriend, Paris, explained repeatedly that he was not dressed as a thug,
but as nineties Justin Timberlake.

Brother Man's picture was an old mug shot, accompanied by a story
that emphasized a criminal charge from five years ago — for child support
nonpayment and tax evasion — and his penchant for false names.
325 Both men's families would say the pictures didn't say anything, that
that's not how anyone who knew them would remember them.

The Neil deGrasse Tysons disagreed over the number of gunshots
they heard; the one in blackface said ten, while the one with a brown
face called black said thirteen. The autopsies would not conclude, but there
330 might have been marijuana in Riley's or Richard's systems, at some point.

6.

I think a cop shooting is too melodramatic when the story was
interesting on its own, and my preoccupation with race is perhaps

292 offending officer: police officer who committed a crime
302 altercation: argument, disagreement
309 excessive: much more than needed
311 Say My Name: reference to the *Say Their Name* and *Say Her Name* campaigns, which raise awareness for Black victims of police violence
313 Spike Spiegel: anime character
314 rectangle (n): *Rechteck*
316 Throwback Thursday: trend to post nostalgic photos on social media on Thursdays
319 bedazzled [bɪ'dæz]: decorated with sequins or rhinestones
319 bandana [bæn'dænə]: piece of fabric worn around the head or neck
319 cornrows (pl): braids braided close to the scalp
320 thug [θʌg] (derog): criminal, gangster
322 mug shot ['mʌgʃɒt] (infml): photo taken of a criminal at a police station
324 tax evasion: act of not paying taxes
324 penchant for sth. ['pentʃənt]: special liking for sth.
327 Neil deGrasse Tyson [də'grɑːs] (born 1958): US scientist and author
332 preoccupation with sth.: constant thinking about sth.

overdone, but it was O'Connor, I think, who said — and I say 'I think' here more as a device, to affect a sort of nonchalance, when in fact I
335 know she said — everything that rises must converge or something like that ('or something like that' serving as another affected clause). But that makes the ending sound intentional or overdetermined, when it wasn't, though I believe — I know — it was Donika Kelly who said 'the way a body makes a road,' or in this case an outline, impression.

***

340 How to end such a story, especially one that is still angry, like a big black fist? The voice is off-putting. All the important action happens offscreen; we don't even see the shooting or the actual bodies or the video. Like that one guy in fiction workshop said, meta is so eighties. The *mise en abyme* is cool but overdone. This is a story of fragments,
345 sketches. Dear author: Thank you for sharing this, but we regret.
    I conclude that it might have been so much more readable as a gentle network narrative, with the cupcakes and the superheroes and the blue eyes and the nineties image-patterning. But I couldn't draw the bodies while the heads talked over me, and the mosaic formed in blood, and what
350 is a sketch but a chalk outline done in pencil or words? And what is a black network narrative but the story of one degree of separation, of sketching the same pain over and over, wading through so much flesh trying to draw new conclusions, knowing that wishing would not make them so?

From: Heads of the Colored People, Vintage, 2019, pp. 1–14.

333 Mary Flannery O'Connor (1925–1964): US writer
334 device: tool
334 affect sb./sth.: (here) produce a change in sb./sth.
334 nonchalance ['nɒnʃələns]: attitude of not caring
337 overdetermined: (here) unavoidable
338 Donika Kelly (born 1983): US poet and academic
344 mise en abyme [ˌmiːz ɒn aˈbim]: stylistic device, story within a story

→ **Info box, Nafissa Thompson-Spires,** p. 33

Comprehension

3 As you read the story, make notes on the following questions about the characters and fill in the table below. Add line numbers or quotes from the text as evidence. Don't forget those on the next page.

What does Riley look like?	
What is Riley's attitude to being Black according to the narrator?	
What are his interests?	
What does Brother Man accuse him of with his slight?	
How does Brother Man feel when Riley ignores him at first?	

Why does Kevan go to the SweetArt bakery?	
What is the idea Kevan has for his art project?	
What is Paris' job?	
Why are Riley's family unhappy about the photo chosen by the media?	

4 Sum up the last two paragraphs of the story in your own words.

Analysis

5 Create a character map of the story to show the connection between the characters.

6 Compare the way Riley and Brother Man are presented.

7 Analyse the story line with Kevan and Penny and its function for the rest of the story.

8 Explain what is meant by 'the constants' (l. 314–315) and what point the narrator is trying to make.

Beyond the text

9 Writing Riley's family are unhappy with the way the victim is presented by the media. Write a letter of complaint to the Associated Press explaining why the selected photo is unsuitable and demand a just portrayal of Riley.

10 a An inquest is being made about the police shooting. The families of the victims and their lawyers, as well as the police officer are present. The proceedings are chaired by a judge who interviews family members, police officers and witnesses. In groups, take 10 minutes to prepare your roles.

    b Speaking Act out the inquest for your class.

11 a Find suitable images to illustrate the story.

    b Create a collage with the images you found.

B4 'Mambo Sauce' *Camille Acker*

1 a Brainstorm foods that are typical for you and/or that mean
   something to you.
   b Create a collage with words and/or pictures of the foods you
   collected in **a**. Be ready to present the collage to the class.
   c Speaking Present your collage to the class. Explain the emotions
   connected to the different culinary specialties.

2 With a partner, discuss if there are (residential) parts of your
   hometown you never go to. If so, why is that? Can you imagine what
   it is like to live there?

3 a **Think:** Describe what makes your hometown/village different
   from others. What is special about it? Apart from your family and
   friends, what would you miss the most if you had to move away
   for a longer period of time?
   b **Pair:** Exchange your notes with a partner. Do you have points in
   common?
   c **Share:** Speaking Present your results to the class.

Read the short story 'Mambo Sauce' by Camille Acker and complete the
tasks on pp. 63–65.

He had good bones, the archways of his arms when he hugged her, the
strong lines of his frame. Constance met him at a bar in Brooklyn. Brian
wasn't who she had been looking for, in a place she didn't frequent. A
black woman in a mostly white bar talking to a white guy over white
5 music she didn't know. She marveled at his views nonetheless, the
intellectual skyline dotted with feminism, prison reform, and progressive
economic policy. The negotiations that night took so long she began to
wonder if she were making a mistake. He wanted to go out Friday night.
She thought Friday was too large a commitment to make. She argued
10 for Sunday brunch. He countered with Saturday night. She held firm:
Sunday brunch. Final offer. They shook on it, and when she tried to pull
away he held on to her hand and she remembered the good bones, the
sturdiness missing from the lean-to men she had dated before.

   He became hers. She owned him outright, paid in full. He said so in
15 the midst of a weekend sleepover.

   'I should post a sign,' he told her, his finger tracing the line of a
rectangle on the left side of his chest. 'Property of Constance.'

   'Is this what you expected?' she said.

   'You're what I've been looking for.'

20   'Exactly?' she asked. She had seen pictures of his ex-girlfriends. He
had dated black women before, he told her that first night. Dated black
women before, sure, but he had never had a black girlfriend—that word
so precious it had been like a child asking for a toy when he first used
it to introduce her to a friend.

1 archway: *Torbogen*
3 frequent ['friːkwənt]
(v): go to a place regularly
5 marvel at sth.: wonder
about sth.
7 negotiation: discussion
to try to agree on sth.
9 commitment:
Verpflichtung
13 sturdiness ['stɜːdinəs]:
(here) strength
23 precious ['preʃəs]: rare
and valuable

25 'Yes. Exactly.'

Ownership had been her lifelong dream, not that he didn't require some improvements, the rickety way he told jokes and the creak of a man who at thirty-five strummed a guitar and told stories about the band he had always wanted to start. He got a new job in DC as a charter-

30 school lobbyist and asked if she would come with him. It had only been six months, but Constance surveyed their landscape, even the rockiness of their interracial terrain, took in the height of their possibilities, and said yes. She could always unload him if she decided to move on, but for now, she was invested.

35 And in DC, Constance could be different. She wouldn't be the part-time teacher and full-time dreamer she had been in New York. She could pursue art, call herself an artist. Brian insisted on it, that she take the time she needed to sculpt and find her voice. Once, Brian had gotten out of bed in the middle of the night, naked and hair tousled, to touch

40 each of the pieces Constance had sculpted. 'And what's this one?' he said. 'And this?' he asked. He came back to bed and she told him, his face close enough that she could whisper and even then, she felt that if she hadn't spoken the words he would have heard them anyway. She told him about her first sculpture and what impossible work it was until

45 what was once only in her mind formed itself in the world. 'You form it,' he'd said. He listened and then asked questions, his eyes closing when he did, searching for the right phrase. And one time with his eyes closed, she had mouthed *love* when it was much too early to think such a word, much less press lips, even soundless ones, into forming it. Now,

50 they said that word to each other all the time. Him, first. Him, most often.

***

The broker took them all over DC, but the neighborhoods where they really wanted to live — Adams Morgan, Dupont Circle, Shaw — were all out of their price range. Brian had gone to Georgetown but told

55 Constance from the beginning that wasn't the neighborhood for them. They finally found an apartment in Far Northeast, the broker assuring them that the neighborhood was up-and-coming.

'I haven't seen many white people,' Constance told Brian after their first visit to the place.

60 Brian said only, 'This place gets so much light.' He fingered the old window casements in the apartment and smiled.

The second time she brought it up, over Ethiopian food in Shaw, she asked. 'And you'll be comfortable there?'

'My king bed won't fit, that thing's old anyway and your queen is

65 enough space for us.' Brian tore off more injera; he scooped up some of the doro wat with the spongy bread. He swallowed the mouthful and after he sucked on each food-stained finger, he smiled.

Injera bread with doro wat

27 rickety [ˈrɪkəti]: (here) awkward, unsure
27 creak (n): *Knarren, Ächzen*
29 charter school: public school that is partially managed by a private company
31 survey sth. (v): (here) look at sth., examine sth.
34 be invested (in sth.) (adj): be fully involved (in sth.)
37 pursue sth. [pəˈsjuː] (fml): spend time on sth.
39 tousled [ˈtaʊzld]: messy in a positive way
52 broker: *Immobilienmakler*
54 Georgetown University: private university near Washington, D.C.
56 assure sb. [əˈʃʊə(r)]: tell sb. that sth. is true
61 casement: *Fensterflügel*
64 king bed / queen bed: US bed sizes
65 injera [ɪnˈdʒɪəɹə]: East African sour flatbread
66 doro wat [dərə wət]: Ethiopian stew

The third time, she finally said it outright because she had to be sure. 'We're the only interracial couple in the neighborhood,' she said.

70 He laughed. 'Connie, how many couples have you seen? The neighborhood is changing. I'm sure we won't be the only ones.' Constance was unconvinced. Brian moved toward her, stroking her close-cropped hair. 'And so what if we were?'

They moved in the next week. Her parents sent a gift card to help
75 them decorate their grand new home and promises of coming to visit from California. Her mother had been surprised by Constance's worry about dating a white guy. Her mother was more surprised to discover she hadn't dated one before.

'I always kind of thought that was you,' she had told Constance. She
80 yelled to Constance's father just then, a *what* that was impatient and harsh. 'I'll have to call you later,' her mother said before hanging up and before Constance could ask what her mother had seen in her. She liked living in New York because she could find mixed crowds and parties where she didn't have to skillfully work her body to the ground like
85 other black women would. As a girl in San Francisco, she hadn't learned to do that. Rock and pop had been the soundtrack to her teenage years, when she was just as likely to sing into the hairbrush of her Chinese American best friend as the hair pick of her black one.

Brian's mother — his father dead since he was a teenager — sent love
90 and a hundred-dollar bill in a card from Virginia. She wrote inside, *You'll get the real money when I can call Connie my daughter-in-law.* Brian laughed.

'How long should I tell her that will take?' he asked Constance. She was hanging their curtains.

95 'Is that the right height?' she asked, but before he could answer, the rod fell to the floor, heavy with its own weight.

* * *

The first day of Brian's job, Constance began sculpting not long after he left, eager to have something to show him when he got home. Four hours in and she had progressed little. She wandered in a circuitous
100 path through their apartment. Brian had a beat-up car that he'd kept in New York, mostly for major grocery store runs, that she could use. She didn't want to drive. In Brooklyn, she walked all the time. One block became ten and she could peer into the open windows of brownstones or eavesdrop on the closest sidewalk conversation.

105 She got out of their apartment and onto their block, the silence of this city foreign to her. She turned onto a major street and was the only one walking. People waited at the bus stop, the Metro wasn't close. Brian biked the distance and he must have gotten stares on his route. The blocks of the neighborhood had few businesses: a check-cashing

72 close-cropped: very short
84 work your body to the ground: dance in a particular way
88 hair pick: wide toothed comb
96 rod [rɒd]: *Vorhangstange*
99 circuitous [səˈkjuːɪtəs]: indirect
103 brownstone: typical old New York sandstone house
104 eavesdrop on sb./ sth. [ˈiːvzdrɒp]: listen to a conversation without permission

Hair pick

Typical brownstone building, New York City, USA

110 place, a Chinese carry out, a furniture-rental store. Then, across the
street, Constance saw a pink-and-white striped awning with script that
read *Winging It!*

Inside the chicken joint, the air felt heavy with grease. The paint
saturated with it. The floor waxed with it. This was where the
115 neighborhood was at lunchtime on a Monday: crowding together to put
in orders for fried chicken and fries. The cost of two wings was laughable,
only two dollars and twenty-five cents. The price was once lower, the
$2.25 written on paper that had been taped over the last price. One of
the women behind the counter was at least in her forties or fifties,
120 another might have been as young as twenty, and a third woman looked
to be in her sixties. Age was always hard to tell with black folk.

People clumped together with no sense of a line, but the women,
especially the oldest one, knew who was next, as if an invisible number
popped up above their head when the bell above the door announced
125 their arrival. The woman would point and ask, 'What you want, honey?'
A short and stout light-skinned man tended most of the fryers, setting
them down into the bubbling grease. The women lifted them up and
drained them. They tonged the freshly fried chicken into checkerboard-
patterned baskets and then held one large salt and one large pepper
130 shaker above the food. Some of the customers, mostly men, simply
nodded for the seasonings. Others said 'Everything,' and then the
women would reach for a bottle of hot sauce too. Constance stood back,
she didn't want to come off as a newcomer. She had hit the tail end of
the rush it seemed, and once most of the customers cleared, it was her,
135 one burly man up to his elbows in his meal, and an older gentleman
sitting on one of the few stools in the small place, and the staff.

'Honey?' one of the women asked. She pointed the same finger at
Constance she had at everyone else.

'Three chicken wings and fries.' The woman nodded and the fry cook
140 dropped a new basket in.

'Best wings in DC,' the older gentleman said to her. He moved the
brim of his hat up to wipe sweat from his forehead.

'Smells like it,' Constance said back.

'Never been here before?' he asked. He had a cane and he leaned
145 into it to get nearer to her. Constance shook her head. She glanced at
the women to make sure that wasn't a problem.

'What you doing over here, honey?' the older woman asked. Her
voice was sly and soft. She wiped the counter down, but kept her eyes
on Constance.

150 'I just moved here,' she said. She had thought *we*, but the sentence
came out with an *I*.

'From where? Over in Northeast?' one of the other women, the
youngest and chubbiest, asked. She had curls under her hairnet.

111 awning ['ɔːnɪŋ]:
Markise, Vordach
112 wing it (infml):
improvise; here also a
play-on-words with
chicken wings
113 grease [griːs]: fat
114 saturated
['sætʃəreɪtɪd]: (here)
full of
126 stout [staʊt] (adj):
somewhat fat
128 drain sth. (v): *etw.
abgießen*
128 tong sth. [tɒŋ] (v):
pick sth. up with tongs
128 checkerboard (AE) =
draughtboard ['drɑːftbɔːd]
(BE): board with pattern
of black and white squares
131 seasoning: spice
142 brim [brɪm]: *Krempe*
144 cane: walking stick
148 sly: subtly knowing,
often to trick people

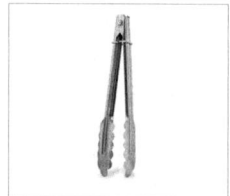

Tongs

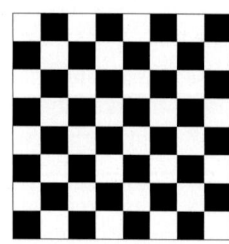

Checkerboard pattern

'No, from out of the city,' she said. The burly man eating his chicken
155 turned with a ketchup-laden fry in his hand.

'Baltimore or something?' the young chubby one kept up with her
questions.

'New York,' Constance said, and then 'Brooklyn, actually.' It felt like
it would give her more credibility.

160 'Where Brooklyn at?' the young girl rapped, mimicking the famous
hip hop line. She laughed and hit the fry cook in the back. He only grunted.

'That girl got too much energy for her own good,' the oldest one said
to Constance. Constance smiled at the ease between them.

'Well, it's nice to see some young, single sisters in the neighborhood,'
165 the older gentleman said. He winked at her. The women dissolved into
laughter. Their shoulders shook with amusement and their heads shook
in disbelief.

'Let me find out Mr. Bruce is in here trying to get himself a young
girl,' the third woman, who had kept quiet until then, said. She was tall
170 and slight, all angles in her white uniform. Under her hairnet, she had
a bun of what looked like fake hair on top of her head. 'He got a chance?'
the woman asked Constance, trying to get her in on the joke. She was
eager to join the sorority.

'He might be too much man for me,' Constance said. She had wanted
175 a good line that was also a little bawdy, and the women loved it. They
responded in choruses of elongated 'Girl' and then 'You ain't never lied.'

Mr. Bruce did his part by sitting up taller on his stool and tapping
his cane on the scuffed linoleum. The oldest one slowed her laughing
enough to raise the fry basket and put Constance's food in a container.

180 'Everything,' Constance said. The woman smiled and nodded her
approval, she sprinkled hot sauce on generously.

'You want mambo too?' she asked. Constance didn't know what that
was and couldn't be sure if she'd said *mambo* or *mumbo*.

'She from New York, she don't know about mambo sauce,' the young
185 one said. She grabbed a couple of small plastic containers full of red
sauce from a nearby counter. 'Try it.' She opened one and offered it to

Constance, who dipped a finger in and put it in
her mouth. It was sweet and spicy, like duck
sauce and hot sauce combined. She wasn't sure
190 she liked it, but the woman offered it again.
Constance took another finger full, and liked it
better that time. She nodded and grabbed two
more containers and put them into a paper bag
with her food. Constance reached into her pocket for some cash. She
195 would bet they didn't take cards.

'Go on,' the oldest one said. 'Welcome to the neighborhood.' She
pushed the bag toward her.

---

156 chubby ['tʃʌbi]:
slightly fat
161 grunt [grʌnt] (v):
make a quick and low
sound
165 wink (v): *zwinkern*
170 angle: *Winkel*
171 bun: (here) knot of
hair held up on the head
173 sorority: sisterhood
175 bawdy ['bɔːdi] (old-
fasioned): dealing with
sexual jokes
178 scuffed [skʌft]: worn

'No, it's so cheap already. I can't let you do that.'

'She said go on,' the tall one said.

200 'Maybe we'll get Mr. Bruce to pay for it. He can't let his new girlfriend starve,' the youngest said. They rocked with laughter again. Constance joined in and took her food.

'See you tomorrow,' someone said as she pushed her way through the door.

205 She thought of ideas to sculpt almost as soon as she got back to the house. She reached for her chisel with chicken grease still on her fingers. After half of the second wing and the huge helping of fries, she couldn't eat anymore. Brian gnawed on the last piece of chicken when he came home that night and told her about his day.

210 'A lot to be done,' he said, biting into some fried skin on the wing tip. 'But everyone seems up for it.'

Constance told him about walking around the neighborhood, but didn't really relay her conversation in Winging It! She said only that the people were nice and that when the wings were hot and just out of the 215 fryer, they were even better.

'What's this?' Brian asked, holding up one of the mambo-sauce containers.

'It's this special DC sauce,' Constance said. 'Try it.'

Brian did, but he made a face after. 'I don't get it. It's weird.'

220 'I liked it,' she said.

'Well you,' he said, putting the small containers back into the fridge, 'can have all of it.'

* * *

The first weekend in DC, Brian's old college friends had a welcome dinner for them. Constance found a colorful dress and wore large gold hoop 225 earrings with it. Brian said she looked beautiful, but when they got to the friend's townhouse in Georgetown, Constance felt like she'd come to the wrong party. Everyone else was very casual, cargo shorts or jean and flip-flops. One of the four women had a dress on, but she was unadorned. The pale pink of the dress was pretty but barely registered 230 between her complexion and light blond hair. They all lived in DC, had ever since they graduated from Georgetown together. A couple were lawyers who went from undergrad to Georgetown Law. There was a teacher, Alissa, who grabbed Constance's hands when Brian said she taught in New York. Someone else worked in government like Brian, 235 and others had corporate jobs that Constance lost track of during the introductions.

They all knew a lot about politics and world events, and made witty and obscure pop culture references some of her Brooklyn girlfriends wouldn't have caught. But the room didn't roll with laughter and 240 Constance noticed early on that there was no music. She was used to

206 chisel ['tʃɪzl]: *Meißel*
224 hoop earring: large round jewelry for ears
229 unadorned [ˌʌnəˈdɔːnd]: without any jewelry or decorations
233 grab sb./sth. [græb]: quickly reach for sb./sth.
235 corporate job [ˈkɔːpərət dʒɒb]: employment in a big private company
238 obscure [əbˈskjʊə(r)]: not well-known

get-togethers that ended in old-school Michael Jackson and hip hop that started with, 'Six minutes, six minutes, six minutes, Doug E. Fresh, you're on.' The home began to empty out, many of the friends saying their good-nights, until it was just Constance and Brian, and Alissa and
245 her husband, Mark.

'You teach, is that right, Connie?' Mark asked. She would have preferred he call her Constance.

'No, she's a sculptor,' Brian said. he turned to Constance and she nodded in approval. 'Sculptress?'
250 'I'm a sculptor,' she said, smiling at Alissa instead of Mark.

'Does that get lonely? Just you in the apartment, right?' Alissa asked.

'Oh, she gets out sometimes,' Brian said. 'Connie brought home this chicken, like the best chicken I've ever had. But then she tries to get me to try this stuff called, wait what is it?' Brian said. He had his hand
255 around a bottle of beer, the other on Constance's knee.

'Mambo sauce,' she said, wishing he hadn't brought it up.

'Oh yeah, we call it ghetto sauce,' Alissa said. She laughed and the men joined. Constance strained a smile.

'They all talk about it like it's foie gras or something. You don't
260 remember it from college, Bri?' Mark asked. Brian shook his head.

'And where are you guys again?' Alissa asked. 'U Street and that area?'

'No. Far Northeast,' Brian said.

'God, no idea where that is at all,' Alissa said. She turned to Mark for his recognition, but he had none to offer her. 'We're so
265 Northwest-bound.'

'Well, your part of Capitol Hill is Northeast. And H Street is,' Mark offered, parsing the sections of the city.

'And I hear Southwest has really been transforming,' Alissa said. Mark nodded.
270 'We like it over there,' Brian said. He squeezed Constance's hand and she limply squeezed his back.

'And it's safe?' Alissa asked. Constance wondered if she had ever been to the other side of the city.

'Of course,' Constance said.
275 'Any other restaurants besides the fried-chicken place?' Mark asked.

'Lots,' Brian said. 'The two Chinese carryouts.' His friends collapsed with laughter. It was a joke Constance had made to Brian after their first week in the apartment, the place filled with too many boxes to think about cooking and their options limited to chicken wings or shrimp fried
280 rice. The comparisons to their former hip Brooklyn neighborhoods had run roughshod over Far northeast.

'And I'm sure the liquor store has a fine collection of 40s to choose from,' Alissa said.

'Not every neighborhood needs to be Georgetown,' Constance said.
285 'Places like this are so,' she searched for the right intellectually damning

258 strain sth. (v): make an effort for sth.
259 foie gras [ˌfwɑː ˈɡrɑː]: French specialty made from duck or goose liver
267 parse sth. [pɑːz] (v): divide sth.
271 limply [ˈlɪmpli]: without energy
281 run roughshod over sb./sth. [ˈrʌfʃɒd] (AE): *rücksichtslos über jdn./ etw. hinweggehen*
282 40 (infml): (here) fourty-ounce bottle of liquor (based on US measurement)

word, 'stagnant. I wouldn't choose a place to live just so I could get an ego boost when I told people.' Alissa reddened, her face now a better contrast to her pale pink dress.

'I thought that was the only reason people ever moved to New York,' Mark said. He took a sip of his beer, but watched Constance over the bottle's rim.

'Well, that's not why I moved there,' Constance said. Brian's fingers tapped out a fevered rhythm on her knee.

'People do lots of things for the reaction they get, right?' Mark looked at Constance and Brian's interlocked hands.

'Like that trick we played on Sigma Chi?' Brian said, moving his hand off Constance's knee to offer Mark a high five. Mark pointed a finger at Brian and began laughing.

'Oh man, and your face when we almost got caught.' They began to talk over each other to tell the story and Alissa stiffly asked Constance if she wanted anything else.

* * *

Constance endured another half an hour until finally Brian seemed ready to leave. They said their goodbyes, but Constance held her face away from Mark when he tried to give her a kiss on the cheek. Alissa told Constance she hoped they would see her again soon, but when she said it she looked as if something sharp and sour were contained in her cheeks.

'They're good people,' Brian said, when they were in the car on their way back home.

'I'm sure they are,' Constance said.

'Then what was with the Georgetown takedown?' he asked. He pulled up to a red light and turned to face her.

'What about their takedown? And why did you tell them about mambo sauce?' she asked.

'What? They already knew about mambo sauce,' he said. The light turned and Brian accelerated, the car jolting forward.

'No, why did you tell them about any of it? The chicken place, my joke about the Chinese carryouts?' she asked. He was driving too fast.

'Why did I make conversation? When clearly you weren't going to?'

'Is this the way we came?' she asked. She peered out at water, but she hadn't remembered any on the way there.

'They're not New Yorkers, okay? But they're still good people,' he said. He made a U-turn right before an oncoming car and the horn of the vehicle blared.

'Why do you keep saying they're good people? Like that makes up for being ignorant. *Ghetto sauce*?' she said, yelling this time.

'She didn't mean anything by it. Everyone says *ghetto*.'

286 stagnant [ˈstægnənt]: (here) not moving forward or changing
296 Sigma Chi [ˈsɪɡmə kaɪ]: large US student fraternity
316 accelerate [əkˈseləreɪt]: gain speed

'I've never heard you say ghetto, Brian.'

330 'Well, I've never heard you be a bitch to my friends,' he said. He pulled the car over onto a small side street. 'I need to goddamn map us back to Northeast.'

'I wasn't a bitch. Don't you call me a bitch. You shared something you shouldn't have,' she said. 'And your friends said things they 335 shouldn't have. Neither of those make me a bitch.'

Brian tapped the screen of his phone, his face set aglow with its light and his anger.

'It doesn't even know the address.' He typed on his phone, then struck the screen, then banged it on the steering wheel. 'We can't even 340 get to the fucking neighborhood, but you want to defend it rather than, for just one night, be nice to my friends?'

'It isn't just one night,' Constance said. She turned to look out the window, the lawn of a house before her, a tricycle abandoned until morning. Silence set in.

345 'No, it isn't. It's a lot of fuckin nights,' he said. He breathed out. He touched the side of her face, his fingertips on her cheeks. 'Of us.'

Constance hadn't been talking about them. She had been talking about the anger at his friends' ignorance, the lopsidedness of feeling defensive and never knowing when someone was coming to knock her 350 sideways. She had said something about their dismissal of Far Northeast, but had smiled at ghetto sauce. She hadn't bothered to defend loving Brian, to question the look Mark had given. It wasn't just one night of excising the parts of her that didn't create the right picture, a paper doll with cut-outs in the right places so that when she 355 was strung up, over archways and doorframes, everyone would be ever so complimentary. It wasn't just one night. Brian was right. It's a lot of fucking nights.

* * *

Constance's second visit to Winging It! was a whole week after the first. She came a little later that day to avoid the rush, and when she 360 walked inside the oldest waitress pointed a finger at her and asked, 'Where you been?'

Constance put her hands together as if pleading for forgiveness. 'I know. Shame on me.'

'See what happens when you give people free food?' It was the first 365 time she heard the fry cook's voice.

'Earl's right,' the woman said. Constance, when she had replayed her first visit, named all the ladies in her head after her girlfriends in Brooklyn. The oldest, bossy one was Gina. The young, sweet one was Joy, and the tall and quiet one was Tracy. She hadn't bothered to name 370 the cook, so she subbed in Earl.

343 tricycle ['traɪsɪkl]: *Dreirad*
348 lopsidedness [ˌlɒpˈsaɪdɪdnəs]: being out of balance
353 excise sth. (fml): cut sth. away
362 plead for sth.: ask for sth. sincerely
370 sub sth. in (for sth.) [sʌb]: use sth. instead of sth. else

A tricycle

'You give someone the best fried chicken they ever laid lips to,' Gina said, 'and what you get? No visit, no call, no nothing.'

Joy shook her head at Constance.

'How about I pay for this meal and the last one to make up for it?' Constance asked.

'Oh, now we need your charity?' Tracy said. They each tried to hold their belligerence, but Gina broke first, laughing off her indignation.

'Come on, what you want?'

Constance walked closer to the counter and relaxed. She ordered fish and asked for everything including the mambo sauce. She'd put some on her eggs one morning, dunked a piece of toast in it the next. They joked with Mr. Bruce again, and Constance found out that the burly, silent customer from the last time who was there again was Gina's husband.

'He don't like to talk, and I don't like him to,' she said. 'It's a match, honey.'

Constance laughed with the girls, slapping the counter when someone made an extra-funny joke. Mr. Bruce said he liked Constance eating lots of food. He liked a woman with some thickness. The women joked that he'd have to wait a long time to get that with her.

'Twig, is what she is,' Tracy said.

'Look who's talking,' Constance shot back. Gina and Joy about died. They slapped each other's backs when they weren't howling into each other's shoulders.

'She think she can come in here talking to anybody any way,' Tracy said, but she grinned through the condemnation. 'Come on, let's see.' Tracy came out from behind the counter and put an arm around Constance. 'Call it.'

'I don't know, think young Miss might win. She got a little more curve on hers', Joy said.

'What about this though?' Tracy turned around, and the women mm-hmmed.

'Now on that back there, ' Gina said, motioning for Constance to turn around. 'Yup, you got her.'

'Give me another order,' Constance said. Everyone began to laugh, even Gina's husband.

'What do you do, Twig?' Tracy asked.

'I make art. I'm an artist,' Constance said, the words dribbling out of her mouth.

'Like what?' Gina asked.

'You take pictures of something?' Joy asked. She posed with a hand on an errant hip and cast her eyes toward the tile floor. She jumped out of the pose just as quick representing the palms of her hands to the room in a ta-da.

377 belligerence [bə'lɪdʒərəns]: anger
377 indignation [ˌɪndɪg'neɪʃn]: anger caused by sth. you find unfair
396 condemnation [ˌkɒndem'neɪʃn]: expression of strong disapproval
408 dribble out of sth. ['drɪbl] (v): drop slowly out of sth.

415 'No pictures,' Constance said, laughing at Joy's enthusiasm.

'I don't know if I can sit long enough for a painting, but I could try.' Joy hopped back to her pose and froze.

'I sculpt,' Constance finally said.

'Like these statues we got all over this city? You might need to move 420 somewhere else, where there's less competition,' Gina said.

'You should do a statue for this place,' Mr. Bruce said.

'Shoot, she might as well make you a statue, Mr. Bruce. Don't know the last time you weren't sitting on that stool,' Tracy said.

'Ain't that the truth. I open up and seem like he's already sitting there. 425 Sleeping upright in there,' Gina said. She and Tracy celebrated their tag-team comedy.

'I could do a statue of Mr. Bruce maybe,' Constance said, hoping for Gina and Tracy's approval.

'No cane though, better to capture me when I was in my prime.'

430 'Who says you aren't still?' Constance said. Joy began whooping in approval.

'We could see your work somewhere?' Gina asked.

'Probably in New York, one of those museums up there,' Joy said.

'No, nowhere like that. Everything is just in the apartment right now,' 435 Constance said. At least this time she hadn't used 'my apartment.' 'The apartment' betrayed no one.

'What you waiting for?' Tracy asked.

'Well, somebody's gotta want to see it,' Constance said.

'You believe in you?' Gina asked. Constance nodded, afraid of 440 chastisement if she shrugged her shoulders or told her maybe. 'You got somebody else who believe in you?' Gina asked. Constance nodded, picturing Brian that night in New York, Brian insisting that all she needed was the time to become a great artist. 'Then you got everything. You bring one of those in here. We'll make space on the counter or 445 something. Move Mr. Bruce over for a few days.'

'That's sweet of you,' Constance said, waving away Gina's offer. She didn't know if they would like her work, if it might strike them as too foreign, as too little, as too much.

'You need something. We can give it to you. No museum in New 450 York, but we can start calling that counter, the Winging It! Gallery. Might as well do it now before we can't anymore.'

'What do you mean?' Constance asked. Joy and Tracy's heads were hung a bit and Mr. Bruce lowered the rim of his hat.

'We're closing at the end of the month,' Gina said.

* * *

455 Winging It! opened in 1968, Gina told her. She and her silent-type husband had watched DC burn after Martin Luther King's assassination.

426 tag-team: one group after another
430 whoop [wuːp]: *jauchzen*
440 chastisement [tʃæˈstaɪzmənt]: (here) disapproval

57

They didn't live in Shaw, where the most damage was done, but they had both grown up around H Street, which had burned almost entirely that day in April. They wanted to do something and they thought what
460 the city needed was new black businesses, people who could show they believed in the city. They borrowed and begged from whomever they could to open and even bought the building.

'Nobody was thinking about this building, about this neighborhood. Scandal how cheap it was and now, they telling us we can get all kinds
465 of money for it. We said no for a long time, but they get personal. They come in saying, "Ma'am, you must want to do something else. You must not want to stand in here frying chicken for people. Who would want that?" Like my whole life don't mean a thing.'

Developers were looking for areas for new condos. This section was
470 filled with single-family homes, not as easy to rent out to young professionals who wanted shiny new amenities without the hassle of a house. The privilege of ownership.

'You can't close,' Constance told her. 'What will the neighborhood do?'
475 'Change come for all of us, honey,' Gina said and sent her on her way with three free chicken wings.

But that night, welcoming change wasn't what Constance wanted to do. She ranted to Brian instead.

'More than forty years,' she told him, shaking a spatula at him as
480 vegetables sizzled in a skillet. 'They started because of the riots. This is how neighborhoods are destroyed.'

Brian cracked open a beer and took a seat at the kitchen table. 'Well, we should go and support them as much as we can before they close.'

Constance nodded, but she didn't want him coming into Winging It!
485 with her. She didn't want them to know that she was with a white guy and that the way she talked when she was with them wasn't the way she talked when she was with him.

'Someone decides that newer is better,' she said. 'People have no sense of their history. And this developer she's selling to, he's done this
490 all over the city. Put developments in historically black neighborhoods, moved out small businesses.' She got two plates down from the cabinet and began to dish up a plate for him. 'I'm going to email some people. Maybe the *Washington Post*, the *City Paper*, local stations, tell them the story and see if I can get something to happen.' She set his plate in front
495 of him.

'You talked to them about this?' Brian said. He began eating, furrowing his brow as he did. 'They want you to stop it?'

'You haven't even been in there,' Constance said. She opened a beer for herself and took a long sip. She turned away from him.
500 'You're right. Maybe I should go in soon.'

469 condo = condominium: apartment that you own
471 amenity [ə'miːnəti]: comfortable feature
471 hassle ['hæsl] (n): situation that requires more effort
479 spatula ['spætʃələ]: kitchen utensil
480 skillet ['skɪlɪt]: frying pan
497 furrow ['fʌrəʊ] (v): make a deep line

'Don't go just because I said to go,' she said, pressing reprimand into her voice so insistently that he would feel it.

'What? Who said that? And you didn't say I should go, you've never said that.'

505 'The point is, it's a real shame,' she said. Constance began to make a plate for herself.

'What's a shame is people burning their own neighborhoods. It's like, why do that?' he said.

'Rage,' she said. One of her aunts had witnessed the Watts riots in 510 '65. She had told Constance that all that love had to go somewhere. Constance had asked, 'Love?' 'I guess you thought that was hate?' her aunt had said.

'Of course. But in the end, rioting accomplishes nothing.' He laid his hands out on the table, open in supplication.

515 'I don't know if protest is always meant to be productive,' she said. 'Sometimes you just have to get something out of your system.'

'Only to destroy yourself?'

* * *

Television coverage was more than Constance expected, but the call to the *City Paper* had yielded interest. The reporter there had mentioned 520 a reporter he knew at a local station. That reporter called Constance and said they could do a live remote the next day. Constance put on a bright orange dress, something vivid for the cameras, and got there just before noon.

'Anne won't come out,' the reporter said to Constance after a brief 525 hello and handshake. Constance turned to Winging It! and back to the reporter, doused in perfume and the irritation of someone with something better to do.

'Anne?'

'The owner.' The reporter began to reek of her indignation. 'She says 530 she's running her business and doesn't have time for some news story.'

'Well, it is the lunch rush.' Inside Winging It!, the crowd was dense, hungry patrons layered over one another. Constance couldn't find Gina/ Anne in all of that thickness. 'Maybe after, you could talk to her,' Constance offered.

535 'It's a live remote. I told you. You're gonna have to talk.'

Constance craned again to see if she could spot Gina. She saw Tracy yelling over her shoulder, probably at Earl for an order. Constance couldn't catch her eye and going inside to talk to one of them felt pointless, casting her voice on too turbulent a sea. 'Okay', she said.

540 Constance dabbed a tissue at her nose and cheek bones, hoping to clear any shine that the camera might catch. The cameraman counted them down to go live. The reporter struck a smile, her teeth shining

501 reprimand ['reprɪmɑːnd] (n, fml): *Rüge*
514 supplication (fml): *Flehen*
519 yield sth.: bring sth., earn sth.
532 patron ['peɪtrən]: customer
536 crane (v): stretch your neck
540 dab sth. [dæb]: touch sth. lightly

brightly, and thanked the anchor miles away in the studio. Constance
tried to construct sentences in her head to make sure she wouldn't
545 fumble any words, but the reporter's intro was too short and the
microphone was in her face too soon.

'And how long have you been coming to Winging It!?' the reporter asked.

'Forever it feels like,' Constance said. The two times seemed an
infinitesimal number to tell her. 'Gina and the girls have made it feel like
550 home.' Constance had used her private name, but there was no recovery
on live television.

'And what makes the food so good?'

'Well, it's the best fried chicken in the city,' Constance parroted
Mr. Bruce's pronouncement since she hadn't had fried chicken from
555 anywhere else. 'And of course, you have to get it with the mambo sauce.'

'And what makes this place important?'

'It's a cornerstone of the community and when we allow developers
to come in and take away these cornerstones, the whole structure
collapses. This developer has done this all over DC and here's a place where
560 we can take a stand against it. They think they know better than the
people of this community what is best for them. We think they're wrong.'

The reporter moved the mic away. 'The developer has suggested a
mixed-use complex, some condos as well as retail. But inside right now,
lots of hungry Washingtonians are getting their fill of this institution
565 before it closes. Anna Bruce and her husband, George, started this
restaurant in the wake of the riots of 1968, and now this city will be
losing a place to all sit down at the table of brotherhood as Dr. King
would have said, with some of the best fried chicken in the city in hand.'

The cameraman swung toward the door of Winging It! just as Brian
570 exited, a greasy white paper bag in his hand, Gina behind him.

'Back to you.'

* * *

Gina had beckoned Constance into Winging It! with just one wave of
her hand and one set, stern line of her mouth. Constance asked Brian
to wait outside, she wouldn't be long, she said. Brian followed her back
575 inside anyway, as if the words she'd spoken had been no more than her
own discarded thought. She tried to stand just a bit apart from Brian.
Not that she was denying him or that they were together; she wouldn't
do that. She just wanted to handle her own business with Gina, explain
that it was like Gina had told her about bringing in a sculpture: they
580 had needed something and Constance had been able to give it.

'Who asked you to do that?' Gina asked. Her hands rushed the air,
propelled by anger toward Constance and the sidewalk that the news
crew had abandoned only minutes ago. Constance opened her mouth
to reply, but stopped. 'You know my name?' Gina said. 'Or hers?' She
585 pointed at Tracy. 'So, how you know what I want?'

543 anchor ['æŋkə(r)]:
(here) news anchor,
reporter in a TV studio
545 fumble sth. (v): have
problems speaking
549 infinitesimal
[ˌɪnfɪnɪˈtesɪml]: very small
573 stern [stɜːn]: strict,
serious
576 discarded: thrown
away

'I just thought if you could stay here,' Constance's voice began to rise, 'it would be better,' she said.

'For you?' Gina said. 'So you can come in here and chat with women who work for a living?'

590 'I told you, I sculpt,' Constance said quietly.

'And live with your white boyfriend,' Gina said. Constance looked around Winging It!, but Mr. Bruce wouldn't meet her eyes and neither would any of the other women. 'That's your man, sister?' Gina asked. She pointed her finger at Constance, her ordering finger, the one that 595 gave you permission to ask for what you were willing to pay for, the one that allowed her to give you what you were looking for or tell you that they were all out of that.

'It's been six months,' she said. Constance shrank inside, her courage fleeting enough to escape her in one short sneeze.

600 Gina lowered her finger and shook her head. 'You think just because you black, you not changing this neighborhood?' she said. Constance's hand went to her hair, feeling for her blackness. Gina raised her finger again, this time for Brian. 'He asked questions. Wanted me to tell him what was the best choice, how he should order, whether people really 605 got salt, pepper, and hot sauce or if that would make it too salty. You came in here like you knew. You thought you *were* better. Just because you live on this side of town don't mean you don't think like they do on the other sides of town. Go save a business in Georgetown, honey,' she said, punctuating the most important words with her finger. That 610 finger ruled the whole place.

'I was helping.'

'You were interfering. I knew who I was selling this place to. Maybe the developer puts a good grocery store in here or a drugstore that doesn't keep its soap under lock and key. I love this place, put my 615 whole life into even the corners of it, but even I know there are better things in this world than two-dollar fried chicken wings.' She pointed one red nail to the plateglass window and the gray of the neighborhood beyond it. 'But you too busy knowing it all to ever figure out what someone else knows. You so sure of tings, how come you didn't know 620 to tell us you didn't move down here alone?' Gina thumbed in Brian's direction. 'Now, I gotta hope this developer don't say no to me, "Never mind," don't say, "Maybe she's too much trouble to sell to and maybe those Chinese down the street might be easier to deal with." Now, I gotta make sure that the life I decided I wanted isn't 625 gonna get wrecked by some girl who doesn't even know what the hell my name it.'

Gina slammed a fist onto the counter. She turned and walked through the doors to the back. Constance and the whole room watched her go. Then the others turned to Constance. She headed straight for the door, 630 Brian stood still behind her. His face was filled with the fire that had

599 fleeting: brief, not permanent
612 interfere: *sich einmischen*

just been on Gina's. Before she could reach the door, she caught her foot on Mr. Bruce's cane. He didn't give her any of his teasing, none of his innuendo. She was quiet too, begging in silence to just get out of the door. Outside, shame and the smell of grease clung to her.

* * *

635 Brian eventually came outside and began to walk to their house, in front of Constance. Her feet didn't bother to catch up, unsure of how deep the water was around her and with no insurance to take care of the damage after. In their apartment, Brian was hushed. The rustle of the bag from Winging It! when he set it down with no gentleness, with no
640 ease, was the loudest of anything.

'Why didn't they know about me?' he asked.

Constance didn't know what answer would be both true and painless. She could find none.

'She made it sound like I was hiding something,' she said.

645 'You never said, "My boyfriend thinks" or "My boyfriend says"?'

'I didn't talk to them like that.'

'It's only been six months, right?'

'I was helping. I was doing my best.'

'People are always lying when they say that.'

650 'You don't understand anything,' she said, but tried to bury the words in an exhale.

'Say that again,' he said. Constance could not and she still could not look at him.

'No, I understand everything,' he said. He walked away from her.

655 Before long, the apartment began to darken. Constance went into the kitchen, wanting a beer or perhaps nothing at all. The chicken, still in its white bag, sat on the table, cold and neglected. It seemed a shame for it to be wasted, but Constance thought it best to get it out of the house. She would have scrubbed her memory of this afternoon
660 if she could have, at least she could scrub the kitchen of it. She pushed the bag into the trash, ripping it as she did. Mambo sauce tumbled out and when she pushed more, the small plastic containers opened. Dark sauce spilled on its journey to the bottom of the bin. Maybe she had never even liked the taste of mambo sauce. The vinegar too sharp and
665 the sweetness too thick. She hadn't been tasting the sauce as much as she had been tasting newness. That was what those developers wanted.

Gentrification was always good at first: fresher produce at the grocery store, a cleaner subway station. Then, a new shop replaced the family-
670 owned one that had been there for decades. The crumbling row house — an eyesore for its boarded-up windows, but beautiful when the first snow collected in the jagged remnants of its roof — is gone and one day to make way for high-rise condos.

633 innuendo [ˌɪnjuˈendəʊ]: indirect suggestion or remark
634 cling to sb./sth. (clung, clung): hang uncomfortably tight to sb./sth.
638 hushed [hʌʃt]: quiet
651 exhale (n): outgoing breath
668 gentrification: process of rich people moving to a neighborhood and changing it, resulting in higher prices
670 crumbling [ˈkrʌmblɪŋ]: falling apart
671 eyesore [ˈaɪsɔː(r)]: ugliness
672 jagged [ˈdʒægɪd]: *gezackt*
672 remnants (pl): leftovers

675 This is what Brian didn't understand: once gentrification started it could not be stopped. And Constance was afraid love would do the same to her.

From: Training School for Negro Girls, Feminist Press at the City University of
New York, 2018, pp. 129–158.

→ **Info box, Camille Acker,** p. 20

Comprehension

4 Tick the correct answer. Only one option is correct.

a When Constance first meets Brian, she …

A is very keen to go on a date with him.
B is not interested in going on a date with him.
C notices that he is the type of man she has dated before.
D notices that he is different from the type of man she has dated before.

b The apartment they find in Washington D.C. is in a part of town …

A in which Brian's friends live.
B they never wanted to move to.
C Constance feels unsure about.
D they had always wanted to live in.

c When Constance enters *Winging It!* for the first time …

A it is empty.
B there are only a few people in it.
C there is a long queue of people.
D there is an average-sized crowd in it.

d The women behind the counter think that Constance …

A will be too posh to like mambo sauce.
B should try mambo sauce because she is new to D.C.
C will love mambo sauce because she is from New York.
D will not like mambo sauce because she is from New York.

e At the welcome dinner, Constance feels …

A that the others dislike her work as an artist.
B as if she has known the others for a long time.
C that the others are overdressed compared to herself.
D that the atmosphere at the party is too formal to be enjoyable.

f When Brian tells the group about their neighbourhood and restaurants, Constance thinks that …

    A he is very funny.
    B the others are eager to come and visit.
    C she and Brian should move to another part of town.
    D the others are being rather arrogant and ignorant about it.

g On their way home from the party, Brian is angry …

    A about the shabby part of town they live in.
    B about the way Constance behaved towards his friends.
    C about the way his friends behaved towards Constance.
    D at himself because he thinks he shouldn't have said anything.

h A week later, when going to *Winging It!* for a second time, Constance…

    A asks the ladies for their names.
    B is told the name of everyone there.
    C knows everyone's names except for the cook's.
    D has invented names for the ladies who work there.

i When the ladies hear of Constance's artwork, they offer her …

    A some tips.
    B a free meal in return for a piece of art.
    C encouragement and a place to exhibit at *Winging It!*.
    D the chance of creating sculptures of the people there.

j When Constance tells Brian about *Winging It!* closing down, he …

    A suggests they should go there together.
    B proposes that they should go to another restaurant.
    C tells her that change is good for the neighbourhood.
    D suggests that she contacts the newspaper about it.

k While live on television, Constance …

    A is joined by Brian on the broadcast.
    B makes a long speech about the history of the shop.
    C makes a mistake with the owner's name when speaking.
    D makes a long speech about the importance of the community.

I After the broadcast, Gina/Anne is angry because …

      A Brian asked her many questions.
      B Constance never asked her any questions.
      C Constance did not present *Winging It!* well.
      D Constance was the only one in front of the camera.

Analysis

5 Examine the relationship between Constance and Brian.
6 Explain why Constance secretly calls the people in *Winging It!* different names.
7 Describe the difference between Georgetown and Far Northeast.
8 Compare Constance's behaviour in *Winging It!* to her behaviour at the welcome party.
9 Assess the consequences of Constance's actions for the other characters.
10 Analyse the author's use of the image of the 'mambo sauce'.

Beyond the text

11 **a** Hot seat: Work in groups. Prepare to all play the role of Constance as well as ask questions.

    b The first person to play Constance sits in front of the group while the others ask questions, which the person playing Constance answers. After three questions, the person playing Constance chooses the next person to play the role.

    c Take turns until everyone has played Constance once.

    d Repeat the exercise for Brian.

12 Work with a partner. Discuss the following statement:

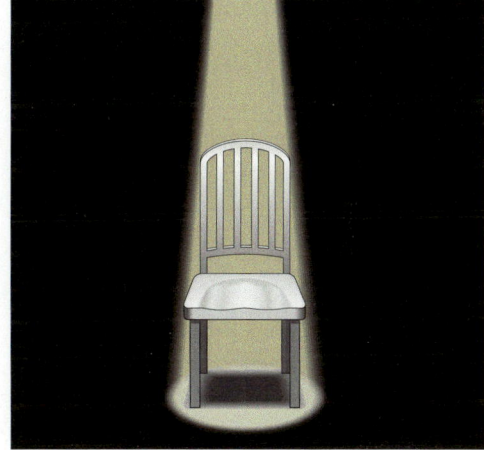

> As an interracial couple, Constance and Brian will never feel happy in their new lives in Washington, D.C. and should have stayed in their old lives in New York.

Part C
Post-reading activities

C1 Elements of a short story

1 a In the table below, features found in most short stories are listed. Fill in the table with the information from the two short stories you read. If the story you read does not include a specific feature, leave the space in the table blank.

Feature	Title: _____	Title: _____
length (can be read in one sitting)		
direct start		
limited number of characters		
concentrates on one character / situation / dilemma / problem		
focus on one single aspect which undergoes a change during the story		

b Based on your results in **a**, would you classify the stories you read as typical short stories?

2 For each of the two short stories you read, find comments the narrator makes and explain how they are used (e.g. to explain more about the characters, to contrast the reader's expectation, to illustrate a point, etc.)

3 Writing Write an analysis of the narrative perspective (→ Info box, p. 158) used in one of the stories you read and its effect on the reader.

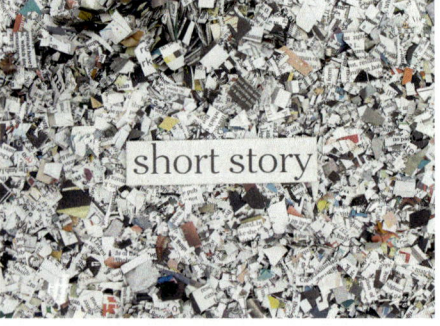

C2 Racism and stereotypes in the media

1 a Think: Brainstorm ways in which stereotypes about People of
Colour are generated by the media.

  b Pair: Share your thoughts with a partner. Together, brainstorm
ideas to counter this negative stereotyping.

  c Share: Share your ideas with the class.

Comprehension

2 Use the webcode on the right to watch the following TED Talk by
Baratunde Thurston about racism and racial stereotypes. While
watching the TED Talk, sum up in your own words how Mr Thurston
suggests that the narrative can be changed.

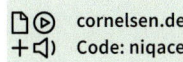
cornelsen.de
Code: niqace

Analysis

3 Examine the way Mr Thurston brings his message across (e.g. body language, content,
language, etc.)

Beyond the text

4 Assess how appropriate you find Baratunde Thurston's way of
addressing the problem of racist and discriminatory headlines in the
media. Do you believe this is helpful/can make a difference?

5 a In small groups, prepare your own 5-minute talk about racial
inequality (in your own country or elsewhere). You can also choose
to record it as a podcast or create a short video.

  b Speaking Present your products to the class.

6 Choose one character from one of the short stories you have read in this
book and imagine they were present at Baratunde Thurston's talk. Write
down three things they might say to him or ask him.

Baratunde Thurston

1) _____

2) _____

3) _____

C3 Discrimination in the hiring process

1 a Decide on three factors that you think are important when you are sending out applications
to get a job.

1) _____

2) _____

3) _____

b Collect the results on the board. As a class, try to agree on three favourites.

Comprehension

2 Use the webcode on the right to listen to a radio report from *wbur* about a study on discrimination in the hiring process. While listening, answer the following questions. Short answers or notes are enough.

> cornelsen.de
> Code: bafufi

TARGET name of a big company
HR human resources
Fortune 500 list of the 500 biggest companies in the world
audit (n) process of checking
prevalent widespread
ambient surrounding
endemic *einheimisch*

a What did Kalisha White do to test if her application had been rejected because of racial bias?

_____

b What did the study find out about call back rates?

_____

c What was in the applications and how were they created?

_____

d What were some of the names used in the study and for which ethnicity were they used?

_____

e What is the presenter quick to point out about the names?

_____

f Did the study ask the companies about their decision process afterwards? Why?

_____

g How were the companies selected for the study?

_____

h How do the companies try to make their hiring process better?

_____

i What was another key finding of the study?

_____

j How does the researcher explain this key finding?

_____

k What does the reporter hope for?

_____

l How did the US Department of Labour react to the study and why did they respond like that?

_____

m What is usually the problem?

_____

n Which advice does the researcher have for companies to improve their hiring process?

_____

o In which industries did the researchers find most discrimination and against whom?

_____

p What are the reporter's and the researcher's conclusions?

_____

Beyond the text

3 a Work in pairs. Imagine that you are a reporter doing an interview with an HR manager of a Fortune 500 company. The study from the *wbur* radio interview has just come out and the company is trying to improve its hiring process to become more diverse after being accused of discrimination. Prepare the questions and answers for the interview.

b Speaking Act out the interview for the class.

4 Think back to the short stories you have read. Can you find examples of racial discrimination and/or stereotyping with regard to jobs in them?

Module II

Pride

Part A
Pre-viewing activities

A1 Working with lyrics

1 a Think: What does the concept of 'solidarity' mean to you? In which contexts do you expect people to talk about solidarity?

b Pair: With a partner, discuss your ideas from **a**. Make a list of contexts you both agree with.

c Share: Share your results with the class.

Read the text of the song 'Solidarity Forever' by Ralph Chaplin and answer the questions that follow on pp. 71-72.

5 union: *Gewerkschaft*
6 beneath: under
7 feeble: weak

((Chorus)):
Solidarity forever
Solidarity forever
Solidarity forever
For the union makes us strong

5 When the union's inspiration through the workers' blood shall run
There can be no power greater anywhere beneath the sun;
Yet what force on earth is weaker than the feeble strength of one
But the union makes us strong

[Chorus]

Is there aught we hold in common with the greedy parasite,
10 Who would lash us into serfdom and would crush us with his might?
Is there anything left to us but to organize and fight?
For the union makes us strong.

[Chorus]

It is we who plowed the prairies; built the cities where they trade;
15 Dug the mines and built the workshops, endless miles of railroad laid;
Now we stand outcast and starving midst the wonders we have made;
But the union makes us strong

[Chorus]

20 All the world that's owned by idle drones is ours and ours alone.
We have laid the wide foundations; built it skyward stone by stone.
It is ours, not to slave in, but to master and to own.
While the union makes us strong.

[Chorus]

25 They have taken untold millions that they never toiled to earn
But without our brain and muscle not a single wheel can turn
We can break their haughty power, gain our freedom when we learn
That the union makes us strong

[Chorus]

30 In our hands is placed a power greater than their hoarded gold
Greater than the might of armies, magnified a thousand-fold
We can bring to birth a new world from the ashes of the old
For the union makes us strong

[Chorus]

Copyright 1915 Ralph Chaplin/ Text, (OT) Chaplin, Ralph

9 aught [ɔːt] (old-fashioned): anything
9 greedy (adj): desiring excessively and more than is needed
10 serfdom: *Leibeigenschaft*
14 plow (v): *pflügen, beackern*
20 idle ['aɪdl]: lazy
25 toil (v): work hard
27 haughty: arrogant

Comprehension
2 Sum up the central message of the lyrics in one sentence.

Analysis
3 Examine the imagery used in the song.

Beyond the text

4 The anthem 'Solidarity Forever' was originally written around 1915 and was re-set to song by Peter Seeger for the film *Pride*. Add one or two contemporary verses to the song.

A traditional telephone box near St Paul's Cathedral in London, UK

A2 Thinking about Britishness

1 **a** In pairs, take notes on your ideas about the terms 'British' and 'Britishness'. What do they mean to you?

  b Based on your answers in **a**, answer the following questions:
   – What are some typical British characters in films?
   – What do you think makes them British? Consider nationality, but also factors like values, behaviour, appearance, clothing, etc.
   – Are there certain aspects of British identity that are unique / are recognized by most people?
   – Can you think of examples of characters or situations that have broken this stereotype of Britishness?

A3 Working with a film poster and trailer

1 **a** Go online and find a film poster for the film *Pride*.

  b Give your first impressions of the film based on the poster you found in **a**.

  c Speculate about the setting, the characters and the plot of the film.

2 **a** Go online and watch a trailer of the film *Pride*.

  b Compare your ideas from **1** to the trailer you just watched.

A4 Background information

1 **a** In groups of 3–4, do some online research on one of the following topics. Each group needs to choose a different topic.

Margaret Thatcher	UK miners' strikes (1984–1985)	HIV/AIDS in the 1980s	Gay activism in the 1980s (UK or worldwide)	world history/ British history in 1984/1985

  b Create a poster or a short presentation on your topic.

  c **Speaking** Give a short presentation to the class about your findings.

Part B
While-viewing activities

B1 Introduction to the main characters

Comprehension

1 `Viewing` Watch the introduction of the film (00:00:00–00:03:25) for the first time without sound. With a partner, make educated guesses about the two characters that are introduced. Where does each character seem to live? With whom? What is their occupation? What are their interests?

2 **a** `Viewing` Watch the segment a second time, this time with sound. In your teams from **1**, each pick one of the two characters and fill in the table below.

	Mark Ashton	Joe 'Bromley' Cooper
Where does he live?	London	House in suburbs
Are any other people shown at his home?		
What kind of interests or plans does the character seem to have?		

   b Exchange your results with your partner.

Analysis

3 Describe Mark's and Joe's appearance.
4 Explain how film editing is used to introduce the two characters.
5 Examine how the atmosphere is created in this exposition.

B2 At the demo

Comprehension

1 `Viewing` Watch the next segment of the film (00:03:15–00:05:45) and correct the mistakes in the following sentences and on p. 74.

   A When Joe leaves the station, he ~~meets up with friends~~ *seems lost*.

   B The onlookers applaud.

73

C Joe is eager to help Mike with the banner.

D Mike tells him he can hold it for the rest of the demo.

E Joe is proud to be part of the demonstration.

F Joe argues that his train was late.

G Mark tells Mike that he wants him to collect money.

H When Mike takes the banner away, Joe continues marching.

I When the woman comments, Joe protests.

J Mike asks Joe to join them.

2 In your own words, sum up why Mark wants to collect money for the miners.

Analysis
3 Examine the reactions of the people on the pavement when they see the demonstration.

Beyond the text
4 a Prepare an interior monologue (→ Info box, p. 36) for Joe at different points during this scene. What is going through his head?
  b Speaking Perform your interior monologue for the class.

B3 The founding of LGSM

Comprehension
1 Viewing Watch the segment 00:05:45–00:15:05 of the film and answer the following questions with short answers.
  A What does Joe learn from Steph at the party?
  B Why has the gay community not been under as much police pressure as usual?
  C Why does the man from Durham leave?
  D Why do they phone a community in Wales directly?

Analysis
2 As the LGSM members are introduced, they are shown in different situations. Find three adjectives to characterize each of the following main members of the group: Mark, Mike, Jonathan, Gethin, Joe and Steph.

Beyond the text

3 Writing Imagine the man from Durham meets a friend and tells him about the meeting in the bookshop as well as his thoughts about LGSM. Write their dialogue.

B4 Meeting a miner

Comprehension

1 a Viewing Watch the next segment of the film (00:15:05–00:20:10) without sound. Imagine what the characters are saying at this first meeting.

  b Watch the segment again, this time with sound. Compare your ideas to the original dialogue.

2 Describe the first impressions the members of LGSM and Dai have of each other.

3 Outline the central message of Dai's speech at the nightclub in no more than three sentences.

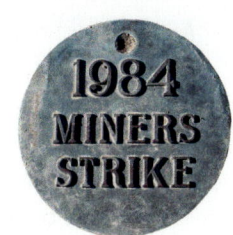

Analysis

4 Examine the different reactions to Dai's speech and what they show about the characters. Focus on Joe, Mark, Steph, Gethin and Jonathan.

Beyond the text

5 Writing You are a journalist reporting on the event at the nightclub. Write a short article for *Gay Pride Magazine* about the event and the new support group.

B5 Inviting LGSM to Wales

Comprehension

1 Viewing Watch the next segment of the film (00:20:10–00:22:38) and complete the following sentences. Don't forget the sentences on p. 76.

A Martin tells Siân to _____ .

B Maureen argues that it's not her who would want to invite LGSM, but rather _____

_____ .

C Everybody on the committee says they are not prejudiced, but _____

_____ .

D Siân speaks up for LGSM, arguing that _____

_____.

E When Martin hears what Siân has done, he is schocked because _____

_____.

Analysis
2 Examine how Maureen and Martin justify their reluctance to invite LGSM.

Beyond the text
3 Writing Write an interior monologue (→ Info box, p. 36) for Dai during the committee meeting.

B6 LGSM's first visit to Wales

Comprehension
1 Viewing Watch the next scene from the film (00:26:20–00:30:55) and sum up the scene in a class chain. Each student says one sentence. Can you create a perfect summary?

Analysis
2 Compare the reception LGSM gets in Wales to Dai's first visit to London. Create a Venn diagram (→ Info box, p. 89) to show similarities and differences.

Beyond the text
3 **a** Split the class into three groups. In your group, describe the event from the point of view of either Mark, Dai or Maureen. Each group needs to work on a different character.
 b Speaking As a group, present your narrative to the class.
 c As a class, discuss the differences between the narratives of each character.

B7 Getting to know each other

Comprehension
1 Viewing Watch the following segment from the film: 00:34:55–00:43:50. While watching, match the beginnings and endings of the sentences on the next page to create correct statements.

1 Even some members of LGSM think that …

A … this is what it means to be gay.

B … all lesbians are vegetarians.

2 Cliff and Dai explain to Maureen's sons that …

C … Jonathan should behave less flamboyantly.

3 Hefina tells Maureen that …

D … who does the housework in a gay couple's household.

4 Jonathan argues that …

E … they would still be in prison if LGSM had not helped them.

5 Gwen wants to know if …

F … he wants to show the Welsh men what they are missing.

6 Gail wants to know …

G … she will not host a gay or lesbian person as she is concerned about AIDS.

7 Jonathan tells Gail that …

H … if she caught AIDS from a gay person, she would nurse her.

8 Maureen claims that …

2 Sum up Maureen's speech to her sons in one sentence.

Analysis

3 Examine at least three prejudices mentioned in the scene.
4 Analyse the means Maureen uses to spur her sons into action against LGSM.
5 Explain how Joe's return home is treated by Steph and Jonathan.

Beyond the text

6 Work in pairs. Work on either **a, b** or **c**.
   a **Speaking** The next day on the picket line, Carl tells a miner from a neighbouring village about the evening. Act out their dialogue.
   b **Speaking** Maureen talks to her friend on the phone after leaving the town hall. What does she tell her friend about the evening? Act out their dialogue.
   c **Speaking** In the scene we do not hear the complete dialogue between Carl and Jonathan as they leave the hall. What do you think Carl said to him? Act out their dialogue.

B8 The next visit to Wales

Comprehension

1 `Viewing` Watch the next segment from the film (00:45:50–01:02:07). Outline what life is like now for Dai and his wife in the village.
2 Describe why the bus is essential to the strike.
3 Sum up Hefina's advice to Gethin.

Analysis

4 Examine the means used to convey the changed atmosphere in the village.
5 Analyse the image of the 'dark artery'.
6 Explain the function of the song in this segment.

Beyond the text

7 Mark is determined to raise awareness and collect more money. Create a poster for his new campaign.
8 a Work in pairs. The scene ends with Gethin's mother opening her door. Continue the scene and their dialogue.
  b `Speaking` Act out the scene in front of the class.

B9 Raising awareness

Comprehension

1 `Viewing` While watching the next segment of the film (01:04:31–01:17:02), tick the correct answer to complete the following sentences. Only one answer is correct.
  a The union representative …

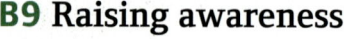

> A is impressed by LGSM's efforts.
> B is counting on LGSM's support.
> C is not sure about LGSM's support.
> D says the men are embarrassed by LGSM's support.

  b When Hefina confronts Maureen in the street, she stresses …

> A the Welsh tradition of tolerance.
> B the Welsh tradition of hospitality.
> C how long they have known each other.
> D Maureen's importance to the community.

c At the recording studio, Mark points out that …

    A there are no gay/lesbian artists.
    B there are many gay/lesbian artists.
    C it matters for the concert if the artists are gay/lesbian.
    D it does not matter for the concert if the artists are gay/lesbian.

d When Dai gives a speech on stage, he thanks the crowd and stresses the idea of …

    A equality.
    B solidarity.
    C socialism.
    D difference.

Analysis

2 a Split the class into four groups, each concentrating on the emotions of one of the following characters from this segment of the film: Mark, Joe, Dai or Gethin. Watch the sequence again and answer the following questions. Find three examples for your character.

  – What emotion does the character show?
  – How does the character express the emotion?
  – What is happening at the time the character is showing the emotion?

b Compare your results in the group, then share them with the class.

3 Examine how the editing of the film contributes to the plot in this sequence.

4 Illustrate how props and costumes are used to create the atmosphere and underline the narrative of this segment.

Beyond the text

5 `Writing` Write a role biography (→ Info box, p. 153) in which you highlight what shaped one of the characters' identity so far. Write in the first-person perspective (→ Info box, p. 173).

B10 Times of crisis

Comprehension

1 `Viewing` Watch the next segment of the film (01:19:02–01:29:46) and outline the events at Joe's home.

2 Describe the problem at the union meeting.

3 In your own words, summarize Cliff's conversation with Helena in the kitchen.

Analysis
4 Illustrate the different conflicts in this sequence.
5 Compare the arguments Joe's mom makes with the reality of Joe's life with LGSM.

Beyond the text
6 Work on either **a** or **b**.

   a `Writing` Imagine Joe and Steph could exchange text messages about the situation he is facing at home. Write their text conversation.

   b `Writing` When Joe's mother tries to comfort him, he does not say anything. Continue the scene and add to their dialogue.

7 a Do some online research about hate crimes towards members of the LGBTQ+ community today. Prepare a short presentation for the class.

   b `Speaking` Give your presentation to the class.

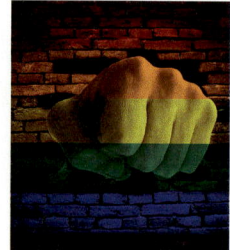

B11 Defeated?

Comprehension
1 a `Viewing` Watch the final segment of the film (01:31:52–end). While watching, write down three comprehension questions about this part of the film on index cards.

   b Using the index cards from **a**, have a short comprehension quiz with your classmates.

Analysis
2 Discuss Joe and Mark's meeting. What should Joe do now?
3 Compare Siân and Joe's moms.
4 Explain what the visit to the hospital has shown.
5 Examine how the scene of Steph and Joe in her bed breaks with the conventions of romantic films.

Beyond the text
6 Create a story board for a possible next scene (after the pride demo) or for a *Pride (Part 2)* film project.

7 a `Writing` Write a script for a radio or news report on the pride parade.

   b `Speaking` Film or record your report and present it to the class.

Part C
Post-viewing activities

C1 Looking back on the film *Pride*

1 Work in small groups. Take turns naming key words about the film. The next word starts with the last letter of the word the previous person said.

2 a Pick your favourite scene from the film and analyse how it is made. Think about the following dimensions:
   - cinematic dimension (camera, editing, sound, lighting, etc.)
   - dramatic dimension (casting, acting, dialogues, locations, props, make-up, costumes, etc.)
   - literary dimension (story, topics, characters, setting, narrative point of view, etc.)
   b **Speaking** Give a short presentation of your analysis to the class.

3 a Work in pairs. One of you is a journalist and the other is Matthew Warchus, the director of the film *Pride*. Prepare interview questions and answers.
   b **Speaking** Act out your interview in front of the class.

4 **Writing** Imagine you are one of the minor characters in the film. Tell the story of the film from this character's perspective by writing an interior monologue (→ Info box, p. 36) in which the character reflects on what happened.

5 a Do some online research and compare the original UK film poster and DVD casing of the film *Pride* with the US versions. What do you notice about the references to homosexuality?
   b Comment on the changes you noticed in **a**.

6 a Do some online research about the real Mark Ashton.
   b Compare the real Mark Ashton to the one portrayed in the film.

7 Margaret Thatcher once famously said that 'there is no such thing as society.' Discuss this quote using references from the film.

C2 „Ist mein Blut giftig?" Enrico Ippolito

1 `Mediation` Your English penfriend is taking part in a project on LGBTQ+ rights. They want to create a website with articles pointing out discrimination against the LGBTQ+ community around the world. They have found the following article about blood donations in Germany, but their German is not good enough to understand everything. Write them an e-mail in which you sum up the main points the article makes.

Ich bin ausgebildeter Gesundheits- und Krankenpfleger. Sechs Jahre lang habe ich in einem Krankenhaus gearbeitet, drei davon auf einer Intensivstation. Ich kam ständig mit Blut, Exkrementen, Krankheiten in Kontakt und habe mich in keinem anderen Beruf so sicher gefühlt. Einerseits, weil mir alle Sicherheitsvorkehrungen beigebracht wurden, andererseits aber auch, weil niemand sich für meine sexuellen Aktivitäten interessiert hat – weder mein Chef noch meine Kolleginnen und Kollegen. Ich war nicht der Andere. Bis die Aufrufe zum Blutspenden kamen. Da wurde es mir wieder bewusst: Ich konnte meinen Beruf ausüben und hätte ihn selbst mit einer HIV-Infektion ausüben können; was ich aber nicht durfte, war Blut spenden.

Oft habe ich mich gefragt, ob ich nicht trotzdem zur Blutspende gehen sollte. Meine Blutgruppe ist 0, ich gelte als Universal-Blutspender, eigentlich ein Segen für alle. Aber es wird mir verboten, weil ich Sex mit Männern habe. Ich müsste lügen, um es zu tun. Was wäre passiert, wenn ich es getan hätte? Ich weiß es nicht, und selbst, wenn ich es getan hätte, würde ich es nicht in diesem Text offenbaren, weil es unerheblich ist: Für die Gesellschaft bleibt mein Blut Gift.

Nun will die FDP-Fraktion das ändern und die Karenzzeit für Männer und Trans*Menschen aufheben, weil es „eine unhaltbare Diskriminierung ohne medizinische Notwendigkeit" darstellt – ein entsprechender Antrag wird kommende Woche beim Bundestag eingereicht.

Fast gleichberechtigt

Zum Hintergrund: 2017 hatten sich die Richtlinien für das Spenden von Blut geändert. Männer, die mit Männern Geschlechtsverkehr haben, durften seit dieser Neuerung erstmals Blut spenden – allerdings nur, wenn sie ein Jahr lang keinen Sex hatten; das galt auch für Trans*Menschen, Sexarbeiterinnen und Sexarbeiter. Die gute Nachricht: Wir wurden nicht mehr dauerhaft ausgeschlossen, die schlechte: Sollten wir Menschen helfen wollen, mussten wir ein Jahr abstinent leben. Wir waren gleichberechtigt – fast. […]

Es wäre denkbar gewesen, schon damals die Richtlinie mit einem Achselzucken hinzunehmen, einfach ein Jahr auf Körperkontakt zu verzichten, um dann endlich Blut spenden zu dürfen – vorausgesetzt, es wäre den Personen überhaupt so wichtig. Eine andere Strategie hätte auch lauten können: Ihr wollt unser Blut nicht? Dann sterbt halt!

Aber: Was zwischen den Zeilen dieser Bestimmung lesbar wurde, war eine Botschaft, die uns seit jeher begleitet: Unser Leben gehört sich nicht, es birgt ein Risiko, der Tod lauert immer, weil wir irgendwie falsch sind. Seit den Achtzigerjahren waren wir sowieso die ganze Zeit mit der Paranoia einer HIV-Infektion beschäftigt, wir hatten Angst, weil wir potenziell in Gefahr lebten, jeder Sexualakt immer ein Risiko mit sich trug, wir hatten ständig nach dem Orgasmus den Gedanken, der Tod würde uns früher oder später heimsuchen. Wir haben immer noch Angst! [...]

2400 Neuinfektionen in Deutschland

Ich kenne die Zahlen der HIV-Neuinfektionen in Deutschland, sie sind mir bekannt, seitdem ich ein Jugendlicher bin, ich studiere sie jedes Jahr. Für das Jahr 2018 schätzt das Robert Koch-Institut 2400 Neuinfektionen in Deutschland, davon 1600 in der Kategorie Sex zwischen Männern (2013 waren es noch 2200 Männer).

Beim Blutspenden müssen folgende Fragen in einem Bogen beantwortet werden:

Gehören oder gehörten Sie zu einer der folgenden Personengruppen?
- *Heterosexuelle Personen mit häufig wechselnden Partnern?*
- *Männer, die Sexualverkehr mit Männern haben oder hatten?*
- *Personen, die Sexualverkehr gegen Geld oder andere Leistungen (z.B. Drogen) anbieten oder angeboten haben („männliche und weibliche Sexarbeiter")?*
- *Transsexuelle Personen mit sexuellem Risikoverhalten?*

Es folgt ein Beratungsgespräch, bei dem die Ärztin oder der Arzt diese Fragen noch mal explizit stellen können, ob sie es tun, bleibt ihnen überlassen. In Deutschland wird explizit in dem Fragebogen zwischen heterosexuellen Menschen und Männern, die Sex mit Männern haben, unterschieden.

In einigen europäischen Ländern sieht das anders aus: In Portugal, Italien, Bulgarien, Lettland, Polen und Spanien gibt es keinen Unterschied in dem Fragebogen; in mehreren EU-Staaten, unter anderem in Österreich, werden Männer, die mit Männern Sex hatten, komplett ausgeschlossen. Auch die „Karenzzeit" variiert, in Deutschland ist es ein Jahr, in Kanada sind es drei Monate, in Frankreich werden es ab 2020 vier sein.

Heute kann eine HIV-Infektion bereits sechs Wochen nach dem letzten Risiko sicher ausgeschlossen werden. Die Festlegung auf ein Jahr in Deutschland wirkt da etwas willkürlich – gleichzeitig bleibt es eine Sache des Vertrauens, denn niemand kann kontrollieren, ob wir beim Fragebogen überhaupt die Wahrheit sagen.

Keine hundertprozentige Sicherheit

Es geht allein um die Sicherheit der Empfänger der Blutspende, so lautet das Argument vom Paul-Ehrlich-Institut, das gemeinsam mit der Bundesärztekammer für die Blutspende-Vorgaben zuständig ist: „Wenn aus einer homosexuellen Partnerschaft jemand fremdgeht, dann eben innerhalb dieser relativ kleinen Bevölkerungsgruppe mit einem erhöhten HIV-Risiko. Dann ist die Wahrscheinlichkeit, sich anzustecken, höher." Statistisch mag es ein valides Argument sein, aber es sind eben nach den Schätzungen des Robert Koch-Instituts auch 620 Neuinfektionen im Jahr 2017 von „heterosexuellen Kontakten" hinzugekommen. Die werden offenbar stillschweigend in Kauf genommen.

Niemand kann eine hundertprozentige Sicherheit beim Blutspenden garantieren, das ist die Wahrheit, so schmerzhaft sie für einige sein wird. Je eher wir alle das akzeptieren, umso mehr kann die Gesellschaft aufhören, einige Menschen mit Scham zu belegen und andere nicht. Die Scham begleitet uns ohnehin unser ganzes Leben, es kostet viel Mühe, sich diese nicht überzustreifen, sie nicht in unsere Körper eindringen zu lassen. Einige schaffen es, sich von der Scham zu befreien, andere tragen lebenslang ihre Narben (sichtbare und unsichtbare) mit sich herum.

Warum ich das alles erwähne? Weil es ohne die Zahlen, ohne die Angst, nicht geht. Und weil ich Geschichte nicht in einer Kontinuität betrachte, nach dem Motto: Früher war alles schlecht, jetzt ist alles besser. Wir wollen vielleicht glauben, dass sich zum Beispiel mit der „Ehe für alle" alle Probleme erledigt haben (ich tue es nicht), aber selbst, wenn wir es glauben sollten, holt uns das Verbot der Blutspende eben sofort in die Realität zurück. Und in der beruht unsere ganze Gesellschaft nach wie vor auf einem uralten, tradierten Familienmodell: heterosexuell, verheiratet, mit zwei Kindern, monogam, unbefristeter Arbeitsvertrag. Das soll die Norm sein. Die Norm existiert, sie lebt, sie bleibt gesund.

Aus: Enrico Ippolito, „Ist mein Blut giftig?", *aus SPIEGEL.de,* 15.11.2019

Module III

Greetings from Bury Park

Facade of a restaurant on Oxford Road in Manchester, UK

Part A
Pre-reading activities

A1 The cornerstones of adolescent identity

1 a Think: Think about who or what has influenced your identity in the past ten years (e.g. a sports coach, a term abroad, etc.). Make a list with five or more of these impact factors.
  b Pair: With a partner, exchange your ideas from **a** and find, if possible, two or more factors you have in common.
  c Share: Share your findings with the class. Then, as a class, discuss the categories of factors that shape our identities. Are some more influential than others?

> **Language help**
> have a significant/profound impact on sb./sth. · have little/negligible influence on sb./ sth. · impact sb./sth. · influence sb./sth. · shape one's identity · mould sb./sth. · have lasting/long-term effects · defining experience(s) · the turning point in sb.'s life · an important crossroad in sb.'s life · the cornerstone of sb.'s identity

A2 Bury Park

1 a Use a web mapping platform and 'walk' through the streets of
      Luton. Start at the place where Selbourne Rd turns into Leagrave
      Rd and head southeastward.
   b Do some online research and find photographs of Bury Park or
      Luton, preferably from the 1980s.
   c Log on to a video platform of your choice and watch some clips
      that show Bury Park or Luton.
   d Work with a partner. Taking your insights from **a–c** into account,
      what challenges do you think Luton had or still has to face?
2 With a partner, discuss which place or district you know that could be
   comparable to Luton or Bury Park. Try to choose a place where none
   of your classmates live.

A3 *Greetings from Bury Park*

1 a Go online and find at least three different covers of the book
      Greetings from Bury Park. You may also look for the film poster.
   b Based on what you found in **a**, explain what you think the book
      is about.
2 As a class, discuss possible connections between *Greetings from Bury
   Park* and your findings from **A1/A2**.

Info Sarfraz Manzoor

Born in 1971 in Pakistan, Sarfraz Manzoor moved with his
family to Luton, Great Britain, in the mid-70s. Since graduating
from Manchester University, Manzoor has pursued a highly
successful career in the media, working as a journalist,
documentary producer, and radio presenter. *Greetings from
Bury Park*, published in 2007 and turned into a movie in 2019,
is his first book. It was followed by his 2021 non-fiction
monograph *They: What Muslims and Non-Muslims Get Wrong
About Each Other*. He lives in London.

Part B
While-reading activities

B1 My father's house

Comprehension

1 `Reading` Focus on at least two of the following tasks (**a**, **b** or **c**) while reading the first chapter of *Greetings from Bury Park*.

   a Design a family tree (see example on the right) of the Manzoor family, providing additional data on the characters (e.g. birthday, occupation, etc.) where possible.

   b Design a timeline which shows important events in the history of the Manzoor family.

   c List the places that are important for the Manzoor family and give some keywords that explain their significance for them.

2 `Speaking` Work with a partner. Each take turns giving a short presentation to outline your findings from **1** to your partner.

Analysis

3 `Writing` The narrator says about his adolescence: 'My teenage life had been nothing more than a failed checklist' (p. 40). Focusing on the first chapter, write a diary entry (→ Info box) in which he writes his checklist.

4 **a** Draw a stick figure of Mohammed Manzoor. Then add notes on his characteristics close to the body part they are associated with. If, for example, Mohammed was an excellent piano player and a devout supporter of Arsenal London, you might write 'accomplished musician' close to his hands and 'diehard Arsenal fan' close to his heart.

   b Looking at your completed stick figure, what strikes you?

5 Explain the last sentence of the first chapter.

Use the code below to downlod a ruler that will help you count the lines in the novel *Greetings from Bury Park*.

cornelsen.de
Code: jetaxu

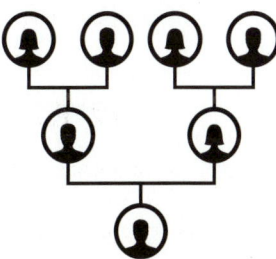

Example of a family tree

Info Writing a diary entry

In a diary entry, you step into the shoes of a character and provide information about a special moment and its significance for the character. This may include personal insights, comments, emotions, etc. Only give information that the character whose perspective you are writing from can know. Remember to always stay in character. Use the first-person perspective as well as a neutral to informal register. You may also address the diary directly. It is common to begin the text with *Dear diary* and end it with *Yours* or a similar formula.

B2 The ties that bind

Comprehension

1 a Reading While reading the second chapter of the memoir, fill in the following table.

What it means to be Navela, a girl and young woman	What it means to be Sohail, the oldest son

b Exchange your findings from **a** with your partner. Are there similarities and/or differences between Navela's and Sohail's situations?

Analysis

2 As a class, discuss the following quote about Uzma and how she might have felt about her situation back then. Consider where the factory is located.

'At the time she was working in the same textile factory that Navela had worked in fifteen years earlier'. (p. 82)

From: Manzoor, Sarfraz, *Greetings from Bury Park*, Bloomsbury, 2008.

Beyond the text

3 Compare and contrast education as you have come to know it to the ways in which children are raised in the Manzoor family. Focus more on similarities than on differences.

B3 Blood brothers

Pre-reading

1 With a partner, discuss the saying 'a friend in need is a friend indeed'. Do you know German proverbs expressing a similar idea?

Comprehension

2 **Reading** While reading the third chapter, collect information on Amolak. Differentiate between background, looks, strengths, and weaknesses.

Analysis

3 It is often claimed that 'opposites attract', but it is also said that 'birds of a feather flock together'. As a class, discuss which of the two proverbs suits the friendship between Amolak and the narrator best.

4 Focusing on his relationship to Bruce Springsteen, make a chart about the body temperatures of the narrator in the third chapter. Imagine his body temperature rises when he is excited about Bruce Springsteen. The more excited he is, the higher his body temperature. Do also label the different events that influence his body temperature.

Beyond the text

5 Looking back at the first three chapters and your ideas from **A1,4**, examine the factors that have shaped the narrator's identity. Record your results in a Venn diagram (→ Info box) comprising four or five circles.

Bruce Springsteen at Wembley Stadium, London, on 7 July, 1985

> **Info Venn diagrams**
> Named after John Venn (1834–1923), a British logician, philosopher, and mathematician, Venn diagrams use overlapping circles to illustrate all possible logical relations between a number of sets.

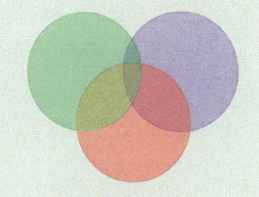

6 **a** In chapters 1–3, several aspects of Great Britain in the 1970s and 1980s are alluded to. Do online research on two or more aspects.

b As a class, discuss how the following aspects shape the presentation of Great Britain in the first three chapters.

the Yorkshire Ripper (p. 31, 2nd par.)

the National Front (p. 56, 2nd par.)

Bobby Sands and the 1981 Irish hunger strike (p. 31, 2nd par.)

Green Shield stamps (p. 56, 2nd par.)

the Guildford and Birmingham pub bombings (p. 57, 2nd par.)

B4 The promised land

Comprehension

1 Reading While reading the fourth chapter, answer the following questions by ticking the correct answer.

a Which of the following films did not make a lasting impression on Sarfraz?

    A *Rocky*
    B *Driller Killer*
    C *Back to the Future*
    D *The Breakfast Club*

b Who of the following becomes a role model for Sarfraz?

    A Hanif Kureishi and Malcolm X
    B Salman Rushdie and Hanif Kureishi
    C Martin Luther King Jr. and Malcolm X
    D Salman Rushdie and Martin Luther King Jr.

c Sarfraz first goes to the USA to work for a company named _____ and his job is to sell _____ door-to-door.

    A Northeastern / magazines
    B Northwestern / books
    C Southwestern / books
    D Southeastern / magazines

d Who pays for his first flight to the USA?

    A his father
    B his brother
    C his school
    D the company he is going to work for

e Sarfraz first visits _____, then _____ and finally _____.

    A New York / Virginia / Grand Canyon
    B Virginia / Yuba City / Grand Canyon
    C Virginia / Grand Canyon / Yuba City
    D New York / Yuba City / Grand Canyon

Analysis
2 Explain what Sarfraz learns from his encounter with the Pakistani couple in Yuba City.

Beyond the text
3 Speaking Work in pairs. Act out a door-to-door sales conversation between Sarfraz and an unusual customer.
4 Since Manzoor does not narrate chronologically, he must employ other means of organising his memoir. Looking back at the first four chapters, explain Manzoor's structural approach.

B5 Factory

Comprehension
1 Reading While reading the fifth chapter, take notes on at least two of Sarfraz's different jobs. What does he do? Who are the people he works with? What does he learn?

Analysis
2 As a class, outline the financial system of the Manzoor family. You might also take relevant information from previous chapters into account.
3 Explain the principles on which the financial system is based. Then explain its downsides.

Beyond the text
4 Speaking Work in teams of three. One of you is Sarfraz, another is his bad angel and the third person is his good angel. Imagine Sarfraz sitting in his bedroom staring at the seventy Pounds he got from Sport Aid. He really struggles to give the money away. Act out the scene so that Sarfraz's inner conflict can be seen and the angels' advice can be heard.

> **Language help**
> Why don't you …? · It goes without saying that you must … · It is imperative that you … · Don't you feel morally responsible to … · At the end of the day, you should … · Why not spoil yourself with … · Come on and give yourself a treat! · You have all the rights to squander the money on … · kind-hearted / humane / altruistic

B6 Better days

Comprehension

1 a Reading While reading the next chapter, take notes on at least three females (e.g. Nazia) or groups of females (e.g. the models in *Amateur Photography*) and the impression they made on Sarfraz.

b Exchange the insights you gained in **a** with a partner.

Analysis

2 With a partner, analyse the different females and groups of females mentioned in the first part of the chapter (pp. 178–198, 1st par.). Is there a pattern or are they randomly presented?

3 With your partner from **2**, analyse how – despite the serious overall topic of the chapter – the interaction between Sarfraz and the Pakistani girls his mother finds for him is light-hearted or sometimes even funny.

4 Work in groups. Imagine you are an English teacher teaching this chapter and wanting to focus on Sarfraz's dilemma: having to choose between a love marriage and an arranged marriage. At the end of the lesson, you want to wrap up the lesson topic in an abstract blackboard graphic. Design this graphic and be prepared to present it to the other groups.

Beyond the text

5 Toward the end of the chapter, Sarfraz muses:

> 'What was so different, I began to wonder, about meeting a girl through speed-dating and being introduced to someone through the family?' (p. 205)
>
> From: Manzoor, Sarfraz, *Greetings from Bury Park*, Bloomsbury, 2008.

Discuss the quote, taking contemporary forms of online dating services into account.

6 a Sarfraz's father claims that Pakistani people hardly ever get divorced - even in Britain. He says this is 'impossible' (p. 190). Go online and find reliable statistics that either verify or falsify Mr Manzoor's hypothesis. Be prepared to present them to your classmates.

b Speaking Give a short presentation to your class with your findings from **a**.

B7 Reason to believe

Comprehension

1 a **Reading** While reading the seventh chapter, take notes on the
   roles of Arabic and Urdu in Sarfraz's religious upbringing.
  b Exchange the insights you gained in **a** with a partner and talk to
   each other about the importance or unimportance of language in
   one's upbringing (whether religious or not).
2 Fill in the following table, focusing on four events from pp. 212–225,
  4th par.

What is the religion-related incident?	What is Sarfraz's reaction?	Does the incident make Sarfraz a firm(er) believer? Why (not)?
mother tells Sarfraz Muslims do not cry over the passion of Christ		
Overall tendency:		

Analysis

3 With a partner, analyse whether the tendency that you
  have noted in the table in **2** is also valid for the rest of
  the chapter.
4 With your class, explain the role of Islam in the shaping
  of Sarfraz's identity.
5 **Writing** Imagine that Sarfraz writes a letter to a
  friend, reflecting on the impact of 9/11. Write this
  letter, analysing the effect of the 2001 terrorist attack
  on his life and faith.

*Tribute lights representing the fallen Twin Towers of
the World Trade Center, New York City, USA*

Beyond the text

6 a Go online and research the fatwa on Salman Rushdie [sæmən ɹʌʃdi] (cf. p. 228).

   b Produce a timeline showing the main events of the controversy.

B8 Land of hope and dreams

Comprehension

1 a Reading While reading this chapter, select at least four key events that make Sarfraz feel emotionally attached to the United Kingdom or to Pakistan, and fill in the table below.

The following key event...	...makes Sarfraz feel emotionally attached to...
A	⚪ Pakistan ⚪ the United Kingdom
B	⚪ Pakistan ⚪ the United Kingdom
C	⚪ Pakistan ⚪ the United Kingdom
D	⚪ Pakistan ⚪ the United Kingdom
(E)	⚪ Pakistan ⚪ the United Kingdom
(F)	⚪ Pakistan ⚪ the United Kingdom
General conclusion:	

   b Compare your results from **a** with a partner. Did you choose the same key events?

2 With your partner, discuss what you think are the three most important turning points in the shaping of Sarfraz's cultural identities in this chapter.

Analysis

3 a Write each of the following topics on a note card. With your partner, arrange the seven topics in at least two ways that make sense to you and that are true to *Greetings from Bury Park*. You can also add an eighth snippet with a keyword of your choice. Be prepared to present your arrangements.

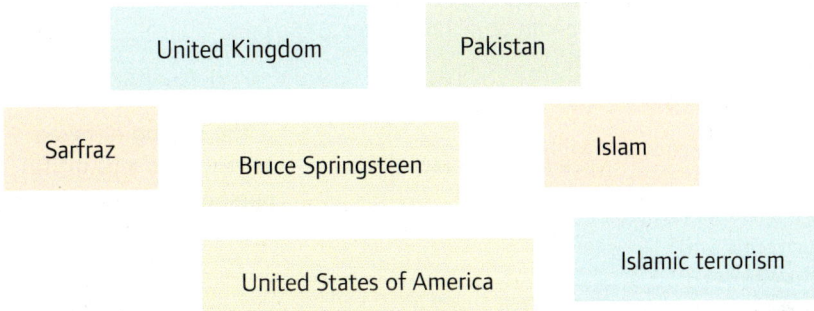

United Kingdom

Pakistan

Sarfraz

Bruce Springsteen

Islam

United States of America

Islamic terrorism

  b `Speaking` In a short presentation, explain your arrangements to the class.

4 Considering the background of the memoir and specifically of p. 265, explain the main differences between first-generation (Mohammed), second-generation (Sarfraz) and third-generation immigrants from Pakistan in the book.

Beyond the text

5 a `Mediation` Conduct an interview with a person you know who has immigrated to another country or whose parents or grandparents had done so before they were born. Ask them how they feel about the country where they live and the country where they or their parents/grandparents are originally from. Also inquire about whether there are differences between the individual generations (if this question applies to that person). Conduct your conversation in a language other than English and take notes.

Margaret Thatcher at the British Embassy in December 1986

  b `Mediation` `Speaking` Return to class and present your findings in English.

6 a Conduct research on one of the following topics (**A**, **B**, **C** or **D**) and, together with classmates interested in the same topic as you, create a digital poster showing its main aspects.

  A Thatcherism and its stance on immigration

  B Enoch Powell's so-called 'Birmingham speech' and its aftermath

  C Cool Britannia and New Labour

  D 7/7

  b `Speaking` As a group, present your digital poster to the class.

Enoch Powell at the 'Birmingham speech' on 2 February, 1974

B9 Afterword

Comprehension

1 a Fill in section **A** of the table below. Which words would you use to describe a beautiful person or feelings of attraction towards one?

  b Then re-read the passage in which Sarfraz sees Bridget for the first time (p. 271–272) and add the words and phrases Manzoor employs to describe Bridget and his attraction to her to the table (section **B**).

	…a beautiful person	…the feeling of being attracted to a beautiful person
A Your terms and expressions to describe …		
B Manzoor's terms and expressions to describe …		

2 In no more than four sentences, give a summary of the epilogue.

Analysis

3 Explain the differences between Bruce Springsteen's and Bridget's influence on Sarfraz's life.

Beyond the text

4 Looking back on what he has learned after writing *Greetings from Bury Park*, Sarfraz expresses the feeling that '… those people and places you felt you had left long behind never truly leave you.'[1] Discuss the quote with a partner.

---

[1]Manzoor, Sarfraz, *Greetings from Bury Park*, Bloomsbury, 2019, p. 276.

Part C
Post-reading activities

C1 An interview with Sarfraz Mazoor

Comprehension

1 Listening Use the webcode on the right to go listen to Sarfraz Manzoor being interviewed about the movie *Blinded by the Light*, the filmic version of *Greetings from Bury Park*. The 2019 movie, whose script was written by Manzoor, was directed by Gurinder Chatha. You will listen to the interview two times.

While listening to the interview for the first time, answer the two following questions:

A How many people are involved in the interview?

_____

B Which aspects of the movie do they talk about (pay particular attention to the interview questions)?

_____

_____

_____

cornelsen.de
Code: tajojo

Vocabulary help
give one's blessing to sb.: give approval or permission for sth.
back catalogue: record of all music produced by a musician
dip in sth.: pick sth. out of a container, (here) pick/choose sth. out of a collection
validate sth.: confirm sth.
tweak sth. (v): adjust sth.

2 While listening to the interview for the second time, answer the questions below and on the next page.
a Manzoor says that Springsteen changed his life again when they were making the movie, because the musician …

    A visited the crew on set.
    B allowed them to use his music for free.
    C liked the superheroes in the film script.
    D gave Manzoor previously unimagined ideas.

b For Sarfraz, Jarvid is a kind of a _____ name.

    A pet
    B pen
    C middle
    D screen

c Which of the following similarities between film and memoir are not mentioned in the interview?

  A Sarfraz's mother's occupation
  B Sarfraz's studies in Manchester
  C Sarfraz's father's unemployment
  D Sarfraz's brother's accident in the USA

d Which of the following differences between film and memoir is mentioned in the interview?

  A Navela's job in Bury Park
  B Sarfraz's father's heart attack
  C Sarfraz's studies in Manchester
  D the time Sarfraz first listened to Bruce Springsteen

e According to Manzoor, what are the two messages of the movie? (Tick two correct answers.)

  A We should never forget our parents.
  B We must not forget where we come from.
  C We should stress what connects us, not what sets us apart.
  D We are united by our love for words, music, and storytelling.

Analysis

3 With a partner, discuss whether you agree with the two correct answers from **2e**? Don't focus solely on the book or film, but also on the messages as general rules of life.

C2 A project approach to *Greetings from Bury Park*

1 a Select one of the following movies and conduct some online research on it.
 A *Ae Fond Kiss*
 B *Bend it like Beckham*
 C *East is East*
 D *My Beautiful Laundrette*
 b Compare the movie you have chosen with *Greetings from Bury Park*.
 c Speaking Present the similarities and differences between your movie and the memoir to the class.

2 Imagine you were to turn *Greetings from Bury Park* into a movie.

  a Who would you cast for your movie? Explain your casting decisions for Sarfraz and his father and at least one other character of your choice. Choose real actors and bring photos of your cast to school to present them to the class.

  b Design a movie poster for your filmic version of *Greetings from Bury Park*.

  c Create a soundtrack for your movie. Select at least eight real pieces of music and explain which of your songs goes with which scene. Do not use more than two Bruce Springsteen songs.

  d `Speaking` Give a presentation in which you pitch your ideas for your cast, movie poster and soundtrack to the class.

3 a Following **2**, you now want to make a trailer for your filmic version of *Greetings from Bury Park*. Describe your trailer by answering the following questions:

    A What would your trailer generally look like?

    B What would be your first frame?

    C What would be the first spoken sentence?

    D Which song, if any, would accompany your trailer?

    E What colours would you predominantly use?

    F What would be your special element that is not in the memoir?

  b `Speaking` Present your ideas to the class.

4 a Go online and watch the movie trailer for the film *Blinded by the Light*.

  b Analyse the trailer and its representation of Sarfraz Manzoor's autobiography.

5 a Manzoor begins each chapter with a quote from a Bruce Springsteen song. Go online and read the full lyrics of some of these songs.

  b Based on your research from **a**, discuss in class which song lyrics fit the memoir best.

  c Explain which line from which song you would choose as the motto of the memoir on your own life.

6 a Using the webcode on the right, go online and look at the exhibition *100 Images of Migration*.

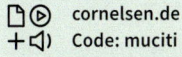

cornelsen.de
Code: muciti

  b Select a few images that you consider relevant to *Greetings from Bury Park*. Be prepared to explain your selection.

  c `Speaking` Give a short presentation to the class explaining your selection from **b**.

A Midsummer Night's Dream

Part A
Pre-reading activities

A1 The Bard of Avon

Info William Shakespeare

William Shakespeare (1564–1616) is widely regarded as the greatest writer in the English language. He was born and brought up in Stratford-upon-Avon, England, where he married and had three children. He then moved to London, where, by 1592, he had
5 become known as a playwright and was beginning his acting career in the city's theatres. In 1594 he formed the Lord Chamberlain's Men with a group of actors, which soon became the leading theatre company in London. In 1599 they built their own theatre, the Globe, on the south bank of the River Thames. After the death of Queen Elizabeth I in 1603,
10 the company was awarded a royal patent by King James I and changed its name to the King's Men.

The famous Chandos portrait of William Shakespeare, named after the Dukes of Chandos, who owned the painting

Shakespeare produced most of his known works between 1589 and 1613. His early plays were mainly comedies and histories. Until about 1608 he wrote primarily tragedies, which were then followed by romances. *A Midsummer Night's Dream* was written in 1595 or 1596
15 and is considered one of his most original and beloved comedies. In 1623 two of his former colleagues published the *First Folio*, a collection of his dramatic works that included all but two of his plays. His sonnets were published in 1609.
Shakespeare appears to have retired to Stratford around 1613 at age 49. He died three years later. Few records of his private life survive, and there has been much speculation about his
20 physical appearance, sexuality, religious beliefs, and whether the works attributed to him were written by others. His surviving works consist of about 38 plays, 154 sonnets and several other poems. His plays are performed worldwide more often than those of any other playwright.

1 a Research the following topics:

Elizabeth I and her time

the original Globe Theatre

Shakespeare's theatre troupes

Shakespeare's family and education

Shakespeare's comedies

Shakespeare's Stratford

Shakepeare's other plays

Elizabethan theatre

Renaissance London

b `Speaking` Present your findings to the class.
2 a Go online and research the Elizabethan Midsummer Night celebrations.
b Your school's project week this year is about classical literature and the Elizabethan era. Using your research from **a**, create a podcast or short video in which you explain the Midsummer Night celebrations.

A2 Lord, what fools these mortals be!

1 a `Viewing` Using the webcode on the right, go online and watch the TED-Ed video 'Why should you read *A Midsummer Night's Dream?*'. Outline the most important themes of the comedy put forward in this interpretation.
b With a partner, discuss whether the short film from **a** inspires you to read the play.

www.cornelsen.de
code: naqici

A3 Love and marriage

1 a Research the circumstances of Shakespeare's own marriage online and state which category of marriage (→ Info box) suits his situation.

b In four groups, discuss the advantages and downsides the concepts of love marriages and arranged marriages have for a couple, a family and society. Present your arguments to the class.

c Today, matchmaking apps or websites are hugely popular. Explain why people choose to find a partner online and discuss whether you think it's a good idea.

Info Arranged marriages

Marrying for love is a relatively new concept. For many centuries, matchmaking and arranging marriages for their children was the parents' privilege. In many societies worldwide, arranged marriages are still common. There are different types of arranged marriages: **forced marriages**, where bride and groom have no say in the matter due to social conventions; **child marriages** (also called early marriages), where at least one of the two people is not of adult age; and **pragmatic marriages**, where the partners have agreed to the pairing a matchmaker or parent has chosen.

A4 Away with the fairies

Reading Read the info box on the Elizabethans' beliefs about fairies and complete task 1 on p. 103.

Info Elizabethans' beliefs about fairies

In Shakespeare's time, people were very superstitious about nature and believed that ghosts and witches existed. They also thought that the world was full of good and bad spirits. Midsummer Night (June 20th or 21st) was seen as a potentially dangerous date because a portal between the real world and the fairy world would open up.
5 One fairy or goblin, Robin Goodfellow or Puck, was especially feared, as he loved to play practical, sometimes cruel jokes on humans. Some of the common beliefs were that fairies:
- were active from midnight to dawn,
- were invisible to humans and tiny (could hide in an acorn cup),
- lived in a kingdom of their own,
10 - could take on a human form and make humans fall in love with them,
- stole children and put fairy children in their places,
- could lead people astray in the woods or cause minor accidents at home,
- could change the weather and let fruit and vegetables rot,
- could cause mischief in households by upsetting objects and interfering with cooking
15 and/or food preservation.
People believed they could prevent such fairy pranks by carrying a lucky charm, keeping the house clean and leaving food and drinks for the spirits.

1 **a** Study the woodcutting on the right that shows Puck on the title page of *Robin Goodfellow: His Mad Prankes and Merry Jests* (1639). Describe how he is depicted.

b The 2022 Oxford Dictionaries Word of the Year is 'goblin mode'. Look up its definition and discuss in which way modern people also behave 'puckishly'.

c Think of representations of fairies and elves in modern literature and in films, and compare them to Puck's illustration on the right.

2 Explain why many people might even believe in the supernatural today.

Title Page of Robin Goodfellow 1639 edition

A5 Speak the speech, I pray you

1 Shakespeare wrote his plays mostly in blank verse, i.e. verses with a regular rhythm of ten beats, sometimes eleven, and no rhyme.

a Viewing Using the webcode on the right, go online and watch the TED-Ed video 'Why Shakespeare Loved Iambic Pentameter'.

b Speaking Work in teams. Applying what you learned in the video from **a**, take turns reading the following lines from *A Midsummer Night's Dream* out loud. Correct each other if needed.

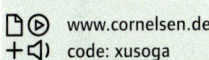

www.cornelsen.de
code: xusoga

> 'Full of vexation come I, with complaint
> against my child, my daughter Hermia.' (Act I, Scene 1, ll. 22–23)

> 'O, teach me how you look, and with what art
> you sway the motion of Demetrius' heart.' (Act I, Scene 1, ll. 192–193)

> 'The King doth keep his revels here tonight.
> Take heed the Queen come not within his sight.' (Act II, Scene 1, ll. 18–19)

> 'What hast thou done? Thou hast mistaken quite
> and laid the love juice on some true love's sight.' (Act III, Scene 2, ll. 88–89)

> 'What? Can you do me greater harm than hate?
> Hate me? Wherefore? O me, what news, my love?' (Act III, Scene 2, ll. 271–272)

> 'Thou runaway, thou coward, art thou fled?
> Speak! In some bush? Where dost thou hide thy head?' (Act III, Scene 2, ll. 405–406)

> 'The iron tongue of midnight hath told twelve.
> Lovers, to bed; 'tis almost fairy time.' (Act V, Scene 1, ll. 345–346)

Part B
While-reading activities

B1 An unruly daughter (Act I, Scene 1)

Theseus, Duke of Athens, and his bride Hippolyta, Queen of the Amazons, are talking about the remaining four days before their upcoming wedding, for which the duke wants entertainment to be prepared. They are interrupted by Egeus, a prominent citizen, who asks for Theseus' judgment on an important matter.

Comprehension

1 Read ll. 20–127 and complete the sentences below.

   A Egeus accuses Lysander of _____.

   B Egeus asks Theseus to _____.

   C Hermia argues that _____.

   D Theseus tells Hermia that _____

   _____

   E Hermia says she would rather _____ than _____.

   F Lysander accuses Demetrius of _____.

2 Using the box on the right, draw arrows to show who loved whom before the play begins.

3 Identify the lines in the text in which …

   A Hermia wants to know what happens if she disobeys her father.

   B Theseus gives Hermia a deadline for her decision about her future.

   C Lysander says he is in every way as suitable to be Hermia's future husband as Demetrius.

4 Read the rest of the scene and complete the sentences below. Don't forget the sentences on the next page.

   A Hermia and Lysander list troubles that _____.

   B Their secret plan is to _____.

Who loves whom?	
Before the play	
Hermia	Helena
Lysander	Demetrius

C Helena complains that Demetrius _____ .

D Hermia assures Helena that _____ .

E To make Helena feel better, Lysander and Hermia _____ .

F When Helena is alone, she decides _____ .

_____

Analysis

5   With a partner, take turns reading Hermia and Helena's dialogue in ll. 194–201. Examine the stylistic devices used and point out their intended effect on the reader.

6   Analyse the means Shakespeare uses to characterise the protagonists of this scene.

Beyond the text

7   Theseus and Hippolyta are figures from classical mythology, but in this excerpt they are presented as living characters. Comment on the dramatic reasons why Shakespeare might have made this decision.

8   **a** Hippolyta says very little during this emotional controversy about a girl's unhappy future. In a short monologue, imagine what she might say to Theseus about the situation and his judgment.

      b Speaking Present your speech to the class.

9   **a** With a partner, think about Hermia's, Lysander's and Helena's decisions and imagine possible outcomes for their intended actions. Discuss which arguments could convince them to find other solutions for their problems.

      b Share your findings from **a** with the class.

10 Discuss reasons why Demetrius might want to steal Lysander's girlfriend other than being in love with Hermia.

11 **a** Writing Write the diary entry (→ Info box, p. 87) Hermia might write on the day before she leaves her home. Take into account what happened while she was in the palace.

      b Writing Write the interior monologue (→ Info box, p. 36) Helena might go into when she debates with herself whether it is right or wrong to betray her best friend. State why she finally opts for telling Demetrius about Hermia's flight.

B2 Stagestruck (Act I, Scene 2)

Reading Read Scene 2 and complete tasks 1–8.

Comprehension

1 Imagine Tom Snout's wife asks him about the meeting of the amateur actors. From Snout's perspective, sum up what happened for her.

Analysis

2 Analyse the means Shakespeare uses to characterise the workmen, or ‚Mechanicals'. Illustrate your findings by giving examples of their vocabulary and manner of speaking.

3 Explain whether you think Quince or Bottom has the higher status in this scene. Give evidence from the text.

> **Language help**
> diplomatic · self-confident · clever · ignorant · warm-hearted · easily led · boastful · enthusiastic · blundering ['blʌndə(r) ɪŋ] · subtle ['sʌtl] · conceited · firm · self-willed · resentful · modest · reluctant · energetic · sulky ['sʌlki] · overbearing · indifferent · uneducated · resourceful · determined · timid · incorrect · practical · vain · egoistic

4 Contrast Scenes 1 and 2 of Act I.

Beyond the text

5 Based on what you found in **4**, comment on the dramatic effect both scenes have on the audience.

6 Outline the plot you would suggest for the following scene if you could choose how the play continues.

7 a Viewing Watch the segment of the film *A Midsummer Night's Dream* (1999) from 00:14:36–00:22:35. Describe the choices Michael Hoffman made to represent Bottom.

b Evaluate the effect that is achieved.

c Comment on whether you find the interpretation of this segment convincing.

d Find pictures online of other actors playing Nick Bottom, e.g. Matt Lucas, Malcolm Storry, Marc Wootton or Hammed Animashaun. Compare their casting to Kevin Kline's. Suggest other actors for the role and justify your choices.

Actor Kevin Kline at a 2004 film screening in Beverly Hills, USA

8 a Writing Write the 'bill of properties' (l. 84–85) Peter Quince needs to prepare for the next rehearsal. Imagine the objects and costumes the play might need and list them individually for each actor.

b Speaking Imagine the slogans Nick Bottom would want to have printed on the front and back of his new T-shirt to advertise himself and the show, and what he would tell the printer about his new role. Write the speech using Bottom's way of speaking and present it to the class.

B3 Looking back on Act I

1 Examine the state of conflict shown in each relationship in the first scene of this act.

2 Discuss what you think about Theseus' ruling and find positive and negative aspects in his behaviour and decisions.

3 a **Think:** Note down what makes a good relationship between parent and child.

   b **Pair:** Speaking In small groups, put together a list of dos and don'ts you think are important.

   c **Share:** Speaking Share your findings in class and add new dos and don'ts you hear to your list from **b**.

B4 Overview (Act II, Scene 1, ll. 1–59)

Act II, Scene 1, ll. 1–59

In the forest around the Athenian palace, fairies appear at night and discuss a severe conflict in Fairyland. Puck, a goblin, tells a fairy that his master Oberon, King of the Fairies, is angry at his wife, Titania, because she refuses to give him a changeling child as a servant. The Queen of the Fairies wants to raise the boy herself. The fairy recognizes Puck as a mischievous goblin who likes to play pranks on mortals, which he enjoys telling her about. Both are displeased that the fairy royals will soon meet there by accident.

B5 Trouble in Fairyland (Act II, Scene 1, ll. 60–176)

Comprehension

1 Read ll. 60–80 of Act II, Scene 1. Tick the correct answer. Support your answer with lines from the text.

a During the fairy couple's conversation Titania …	Line(s):
A accuses Oberon of being unfaithful.	
B asks the fairies to stay and protect her.	_____
C criticizes Oberon for wanting to steal the changeling boy.	
b Oberon says that …	Line(s):
A he wants Titania to leave immediately.	
B Titania herself had an affair with another man.	_____
C he no longer considers himself Titania's husband.	

2 Now read ll. 81–117 of the scene. In her speech, Titania lists changes in nature caused by her and Oberon's quarrelling. Sum up the main points/consequences mentioned in her weather report in the table below.

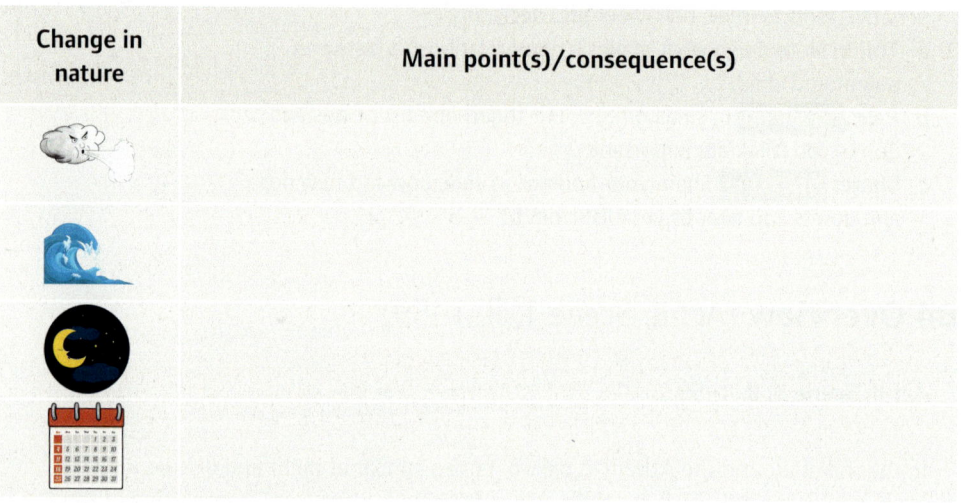

Change in nature	Main point(s)/consequence(s)

3 Read ll. 118–187 of the scene. The action is summed up in statements A–G in the table below. Put them in the correct order by writing numbers 1–7 in the right column.

Statement	Order
A Puck leaves to carry out Oberon's order.	
B Oberon decides to punish his wife for her refusal to grant him his wish.	
C Titania explains her reasons for keeping the changeling boy.	
D Oberon tells Puck about the magic powers of a little flower.	
E Oberon outlines his scheme to trick Titania into doing what he wants.	
F Oberon asks Titania to give up the changeling boy.	
G Titania invites Oberon to join her and her fairies.	

Analysis
4 Examine the dramatic function of the passages dealt with in tasks **2** and **3**.

5 a Read Oberon's speech in ll. 176–187 and try out different ways of speaking it, e.g. sarcastically, angrily or full of glee.

b Speaking Decide which attitude fits which part best and perform the speech in a dramatic reading to the class.

Beyond the text

6 a Though the changeling boy is not listed among the characters, many directors have chosen to put him onstage when Titania and Oberon are fighting about him. Create a design for the changeling boy in this scene and draw a sketch of the character.

b Discuss the theatrical function of the changeling boy's role and how the audience's response to the scene could change if he were actually present.

c Speculate on possible reasons why Oberon wants to take the child from Titania.

d If you had to give custody of the boy to either Titania or Oberon, which one would you choose? Discuss with a partner.

7 Writing Nowadays, Titania would have reason to accuse mankind of bringing chaos into the natural world. State the most important current manmade environmental issues and their effect on our lives. Write the speech she would give to global leaders to persuade them to take more efficient action.

B6 Fool for love (Act II, Scene 1, ll. 176–268)

Reading Read the rest of Scene 1 and complete tasks 1–6.

Comprehension

1 Correct the mistakes in the following sentences.

A Oberon is planning to send a forest animal to attack Titania.

B Demetrius regrets that he cannot love Helena in return.

C Helena is worried that Demetrius might harm her.

D Oberon plans to smear Demetrius' eyes with the love juice.

2 Use arrows in the box on the right to show who loves whom when entering the woods.

Who loves whom?
Entering the woods

Hermia	Helena
Lysander	Demetrius

Analysis

3 a Viewing Using the webcode on the right, go online and watch the Royal Shakespeare Company's video 'Exploring a Duologue' from the series *The Text Detectives*.

www.cornelsen.de
code: paduho

b Apply what is said in the video about shared language, questions and answers as well as names and status to your reading of Demetrius' and Helena's duologue (ll. 188–244). Illustrate your findings with several examples.

4 Analyse the imagery used in Oberon's description of Titania's resting place and his plan of action. Point out the effect which is created (ll. 248–258).

Beyond the text

5 a Think: Think about your personal reaction to the way Helena pleads with Demetrius.

b Pair: `Speaking` With a partner, exchange your ideas from **a** and find reasons why she might behave like she does.

c Share: `Speaking` Share your findings with the class. As a class, discuss more realistic ways to help Helena solve her dilemma than Oberon's use of magic.

6 a Create a costume and stage design for the fairy world in the Athenian woods that captures the spirit of the place as described in the text.

b `Speaking` Present your creations in a gallery walk activity. Explain your choice for the fairy costumes and the intended overall effect of your concept on the audience.

B7 Spellbound (Act II, Scene 2)

`Reading` Read Scene 2 and complete tasks 1–7.

Comprehension

1 Divide the dialogue into sense units which match the headings in the table below. Number the headings in the correct order and add the line numbers on the right.

Heading	Order	Line(s)
A Mission accomplished		
B A nightmare come true		
C A little night music		
D Single beds		
E A man transformed		
F A wicked spell		

2 Use arrows in the box on the right to show who loves whom after the first love juice has been applied.

Analysis
3 a Analyse the rhythm of Puck's speech in ll. 66–83, comparing it to the metre used by the mortals in this scene.
   b Explain the effect Puck's lines have.
4 Examine the effect the frequent change of pace has in this scene.
5 a At the end of this scene, both Helena and Hermia are troubled. Read what they say in ll. 123–134 and ll. 145–156 and compare their sorrows.
   b Discuss which predicament you find worse.

Beyond the text
6 a Imagine Puck has several Puck clones with him that are acting as a chorus. Prepare a dramatic reading of the passage with one of you reading Puck and the others echoing key words or making fitting sounds to enhance the overall effect.
   b <mark>Speaking</mark> Present your dramatic reading of the passage to the class.
7 a Imagine you were asked to set Titania's lullaby to music for your school's production of the play. Find suitable music and prepare to explain your choice.
   b <mark>Speaking</mark> Present your music to the class.

Who loves whom?

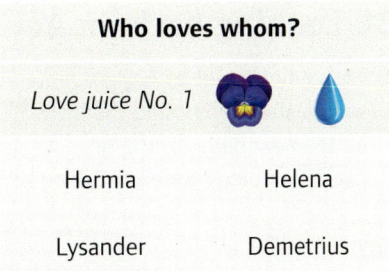

Love juice No. 1		
Hermia		Helena
Lysander		Demetrius

B8 Looking back on Act II

1 The complex plot of *A Midsummer Night's Dream* can be followed and illustrated by using the icons from the key below. Fill in the table on the next page for the first two acts with little icon drawings and continue doing so while working on the rest of the play.

Key:

in the scene	E elopes	uses love juice	F foul: attacks someone	goes on a hunt
in love	quarrels	uses spell	is transformed	marries
suffers heartbreak	rehearses / performs play	uses antidote	has a dream	dies a stage death

2 **a** In four groups, describe the setting, the environment, the characters, the social status and the rules of the four worlds, i.e. the Court, the Lovers, the Mechanicals and the Fairies. Each group looks at one of the four worlds.

 b Create a meme reflecting the spirit of the people of the world your group worked on and design a coat of arms or badge they would want to have.

3 Explain the way both themes of *Men controlling women* as well as *Women defying men* are represented in Acts I and II.

B9 A donkey lover (Act III, Scene 1)

Reading Read Scene 1 and complete tasks 1–7.

Comprehension

1 Speaking Imagine a curious neighbour has followed the Mechanicals into the woods, observed their rehearsal and then ran away with the others. In a one-minute talk, summarise what the neighbour would tell their friends about the nightly events (ll. 1–100).

2 Writing Imagine a fairy who has watched Puck's prank wants to post the information on his latest mischief on her blog *puck.fandom*. Write her blog entry in which she sums up what happens in ll. 101–177.

	Act I, Scene 1	Act I, Scene 2	Act II, Scene 1	Act II, Scene 2	Act III, Scene 1	Act III, Scene 2	Act IV, Scene 1	Act IV, Scene 2	Act V, Scene 1
Theseus									
Hippolyta									
Philostrate									
Egeus									
Hermia									
Helena									
Lysander									
Demetrius									
Oberon									
Titania									
Puck									
Fairies									
Quince									
Bottom									
Flute									
Snout									
Snug									
Starveling									

Analysis

3 Compare Titania's declaration of love to Bottom in this scene with what Helena says to Demetrius about her feelings for him in Act II, Scene 1, ll. 195–244.

Beyond the text

4 Discuss what the Mechanicals misunderstand about the nature of theatrical illusion.

5 Change plays a big role in this scene. Evaluate the effect Shakespeare achieved with this dramaturgical device.

6 Discuss why Bottom's statement that 'Reason and love keep little company together nowadays' (ll. 122–123) is apt at this point in the play but also true for characters shown in Acts I and II.

7 A member of your school's drama group needs advice: They want to design a donkey's head for their production of *A Midsummer Night's Dream*, but it cannot hide the actor's face nor be too overdone. Discuss your ideas with a partner.

B10 Overview (Act III, Scene 2, ll. 1–40)

Act III, Scene 2, ll. 1–40

Wondering if his love juice has already worked on Titania, Oberon is delighted to hear from Puck that she is now in love with a 'monster', a man with a donkey's head. His servant also spread the juice on a man wearing Athenian clothes, as he was instructed to do.

B11 Love triangle (Act III, Scene 2, ll. 41–377)

Comprehension

1 a Read the passage which describes the meeting of all four lovers (ll. 41–377). Fill in the table below with a suitable heading for each section. The first one has already been done for you as an example. Don't forget the ones on the next page.

Section	Heading
A ll. 41–87	A serious accusation
B ll. 88–121	
C ll.122–176	

D ll. 177–281

E ll. 282–344

F ll. 345–377

b Use arrows in the box on the right to show who loves whom after the second love juice has been applied.

c Outline each of the four lovers' problems and conflicting aims at this point in the play.

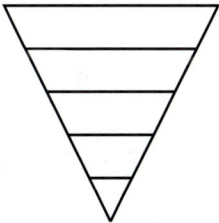

Who loves whom?	
Love juice No. 2 🌼 💧	
Hermia	Helena
Lysander	Demetrius

Analysis

2 a Compare the language Lysander uses when declaring his love for Helena and when rejecting Hermia.

b Rank the insults Lysander directs at Hermia from least to most hurtful (ll. 258–330). Use an inverted pyramid diagram with the most offensive remark placed at the top.

3 While both Oberon and Puck are onstage and invisible, they observe the lovers' quarrel. Think about ways their presence could be made interesting to the audience. Draw a bird's eye view diagram of all characters' placement and movement throughout the scene.

Beyond the text

4 Discuss who you feel the most sympathy for in this scene.

> **Language help**
> deceived/betrayed/cheated · drugged [drʌgd] · mocked/ridiculed · jealous · helpless · regret/feel sorry for · furious · humiliated/scorned [skɔːnd] · disappointed · offended/insulted · feel pity for sb./sth. · rejected/jilted [dʒɪltɪd] · be outraged by sb./sth. · desperate · determined · overwhelmed

5 a `Viewing` Using the webcode on the right, go online and listen to the song 'Chasing my Tail' from the 2022 musical *The Lovers*, which illustrates Helena's romantic dilemma. Note down the main points made in the song.

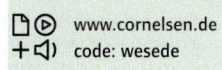

www.cornelsen.de
code: wesede

b `Writing` Write the song lyrics Hermia could sing to describe her experiences in this scene.

6 a Imagine Oberon had to defend his actions in front of an ethics committee that challenges his decisions. Prepare Oberon's justifications and the questions he could be asked about his treatment of Titania and the lovers.

b `Speaking` Stage the interview with one student being Oberon and the rest of the class being his interrogators. Take turns playing Oberon in the hot seat.

B12 Overview (Act III, Scene 2, ll. 278–463)

Act III, Scene 2, ll. 278–463

Puck realises that he must hurry to carry out his orders because dawn is approaching. He spreads fog in the woods to stop Lysander and Demetrius from duelling. Then he leads all four lovers astray. They are all so confused and exhausted that they lie down and sleep on the ground. Finally, Puck squeezes the antidote to the love juice on Lysander's eyes to release him from the magic spell.

B13 Looking back on Act III

1 Use arrows in the box on the right to show who loves whom after the third love juice has been applied.

2 a In three big groups, examine how the themes of *Disorder and harmony, Gender roles* and *Contrast* are dealt with in Acts I-III. Each group works on one theme.
b Share your findings with the rest of the class.

3 a Writing The characters in *A Midsummer Night's Dream* are not fully rounded, but rather stock characters or stereotypes with a particular function. Write mini portraits of all characters.
b Explain why Shakespeare might have chosen this way of representation.

4 a Create an atmospheric soundscape for this enchanted forest with fairy, nature and animal sounds as well as the noises the people who went there make. Think about how the magic spell moment could have a very theatrical effect.
b Play your audio file to the class.

Who loves whom?		
Love juice No. 3	🌱	💧
Hermia		Helena
Lysander		Demetrius

B14 The fierce vexation of a dream (Act IV. Scene 1)

Reading Read Scene 1 and complete tasks 1–5.

Comprehension

1 Match the sentence halves on the next page to create correct statements.

1 Bottom enjoys being spoiled by the fairies …

A … but doesn't realize that he is under a love spell.

2 Titania is reconciled with Oberon …

B … but is overruled by Theseus.

3 Egeus demands Lysander's punishment …

C … but they are ready to follow Theseus back to Athens.

4 Demetrius says he loves Helena again …

D … but cannot put it into words when he is awake.

5 The lovers are confused about what happened during the night …

E …. but has given up the changeling boy while under his spell.

Analysis

2 Examine the means used to highlight Bottom's 'donkeyness' in ll. 1–43.

3 Analyse the dramatic function of this scene.

4 Using a Venn diagram with three circles (→ Info box, p. 89), compare the reactions of the characters who have woken up: Titania, Bottom and the lovers. The very centre of the diagram contains what all six characters have in common.

Beyond the text

5 Writing Write a new scene in modern English in which Oberon tells Titania how she was found sleeping alongside mortals on the ground. Decide how truthful he is going to be.

B15 Overview (Act IV, Scene 2)

Act IV, Scene 2

The Mechanicals have returned to Athens and are frustrated because they cannot find Bottom, without whom their play cannot be performed. Snug tells them that Theseus and other lords and ladies have gotten married. Suddenly Bottom appears without telling them where he was and announces that their play was 'preferred' for the wedding ceremony. He organizes their preparations quickly and they all leave for the palace.

B16 Looking back on Act IV

1 In order to define the relationships between the characters in *A Midsummer Night's Dream*, match the numbers of the following organigram to the descriptions listed below it. Use the box at the bottom of the page to write your answers.

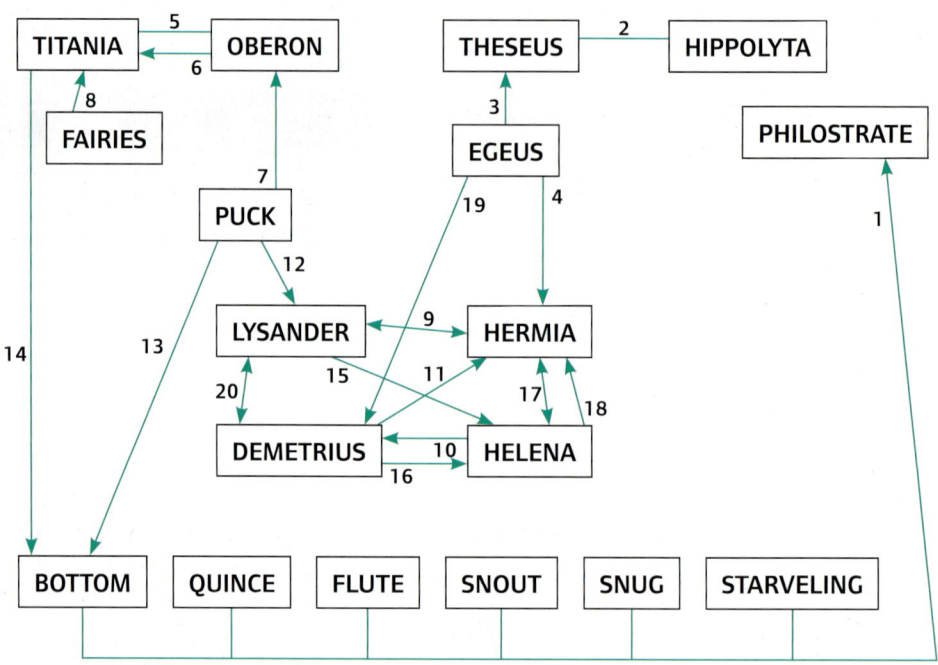

a has the parental support to marry   **b** temporarily loves   **c** serve   **d** asks for help
e remains under the love spell   **f** best friends   **g** serves   **h** transforms into another being
i betrays of trust   **j** father to   **k** engaged   **l** hired by   **m** married   **n** unhappily in love with
o in true love   **p** rivals   **q** prefers   **r** mistakes him for someone else   **s** takes revenge on
t has sex with

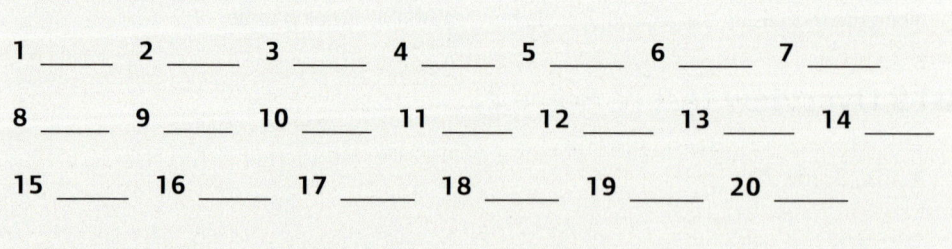

| 1 ____ | 2 ____ | 3 ____ | 4 ____ | 5 ____ | 6 ____ | 7 ____ |

| 8 ____ | 9 ____ | 10 ____ | 11 ____ | 12 ____ | 13 ____ | 14 ____ |

| 15 ____ | 16 ____ | 17 ____ | 18 ____ | 19 ____ | 20 ____ |

2 Analyse how the theme *Dream, illusion and reality* is treated in Acts II – IV.

3 **Viewing** Watch the segments of the film *A Midsummer Night's Dream* (1999) from 00:23:36–00:30:15 and 00:55:30–00:58:19. Describe the fairy world and the fairies the director has added to the cast. Discuss the effect that is achieved.

4 **Writing** Create an AI chatbot fairy character with an online software such as *Inworld* or *Beta Character AI* and strike up a chat conversation about fairies with it.

5 Refer back to your descriptions of the four worlds (**B8, 2a**, p. 112) and continue working in the same groups to outline the changes each world and its characters have undergone as well as their mutual interaction up to the end of Act IV.

B17 Overview (Act V, Scene 1, ll. 1–105)

Act V, Scene 1, ll. 1–105

In the palace, Theseus and Hippolyta discuss what the lovers have told them about their experiences in the forest. While Hippolyta believes them, Theseus is sceptical because love and imagination can create delusions - especially for people with overactive brains like lovers, poets and madmen. After the lovers have joined them, Theseus asks his Master of the Revels, Philostrate, what entertainment is available and dismisses all offerings but the workman's play which promises 'very tragical mirth' in a 'tedious and brief' show. Despite Philostrate's insistence that the actors are terrible, Theseus orders them to perform because he thinks good intentions matter more than competence.

B18 Send in the clowns (Act V. Scene 1. ll. 106–420)

Comprehension

1 Read the rest of the scene and complete the sentences below. Don't forget the ones on the next page.

A Understanding Quince's first ten lines is difficult because _____

_____ .

B In the rest of the prologue, Quince _____ .

C Snout as the Wall tells his audience that _____ .

D Bottom and Flute, separated by the Wall, speak about _____

_____ .

E Snug and Starveling enter to explain that _____

_____ .

F Theseus and the lovers continuously _____ .

G Bottom and Flute, passing as Pyramus and Thisbe, both _____ .

H After the court has retired to bed, _____ .

Analysis

2 Examine the function and the dramatic impact of the play-within-the-play.

3 Draw a seating and movement sketch map for the performance of *Pyramus and Thisbe* which allows for interaction between the actors and their onstage audience, and ensures that the real theatre audience can see the full cast throughout.

Beyond the text

4 a `Viewing` Watch the performance of *Pyramus and Thisbe* in Hoffman's film (01:33:18–01:46:03).

  b Examine the means the filmmakers used to create comedy and assess whether they have achieved their aim.

  c `Speaking` Stage your own dramatization of Quince's prologue (ll. 126–150) with much comic business for Wall, Lion, Moonshine and the tragic lovers.

5 a `Writing` Write a play review of the Mechanicals' version of *Pyramus and Thisbe* from Philostrate's perspective (→ Info box, Writing a film/play review, p. 154). Comment on the actors' performances, the text of the play, its scenery and props and include the audience's reaction to the show. Add a rating and a recommendation to your article.

  b Imagine a reporter asks Quince for an interview after the show. With a partner, find suitable questions and replies, e.g. for
    – how Quince thought the play was received,
    – what he thought of his actors' performances,
    – what his plans are for the next play.

  c `Speaking` Practice the dialogue and perform it for the class.

  d Design the poster and programme the Mechanicals could have created for their performance of *Pyramus and Thisbe*. Include the actors' biographies, the parts they are playing, a plot synopsis that does not reveal the ending and a special thanks to Theseus.

B19 Looking back on Act V

1 Examine the function and importance of the forest as opposed to the city of Athens as the place of action for most of the play, including the fairies' visit to the palace at the end.

2 **a** Shakespeare pokes fun at amateur theatre groups. Illustrate the instances of bad acting shown in Act III, Scene 1 and Act V, Scene 1.
 b Discuss what you consider to be qualities of good acting.

3 *A Midsummer Night's Dream* contains comedy on several levels. Analyse the comic aspects of characters, action and language.

B20 Looking back at the drama

1 **a** Viewing Using the webcode on the right, go online and watch the TED-Ed video 'Should you care what your parents think?' about the so-called 'Romeo and Juliet effect'.

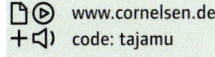
www.cornelsen.de
code: tajamu

 b With a partner, discuss the points made in the film.

2 Writing Imagine you want to play a role in your school's English language production of *A Midsummer Night's Dream*. Choose the part you want to audition for and write an email to the director of the play in which you explain your choice and why you think you would be perfect for it.

3 **a** As a class, create a human continuum – form a human line of argument from 'totally agree' to 'totally disagree' – according to your views on Samuel Pepys' review of *A Midsummer Night's Dream*.

> *To the King's Theatre, where we saw* Midsummer's nights Dreame, *which I have never seen before, nor shall ever again, for it is the most insipid ridiculous play that ever I saw in my life. I saw, I confess, some good dancing and some handsome women, which was all my pleasure.*
>
> Samuel Pepys, *Diary*, September 29, 1662

 b Comment on your decision and to what extent you agree with Pepys' opinion. Discuss if young people today can still relate to the play.

Part C
Post-reading activities

C1 Themes

1 a Love and marriage are essential themes that are reflected in nearly all relationships of *A Midsummer Night's Dream*. Think of the characters, couples and dramatic elements the themes of love and marriage relate to and write your findings next to the arrowheads in the two diagrams.

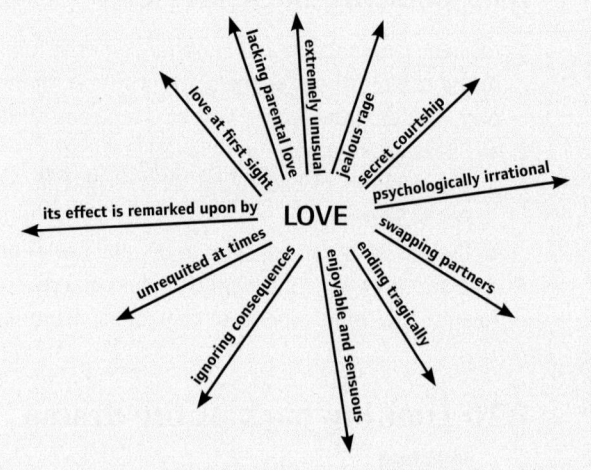

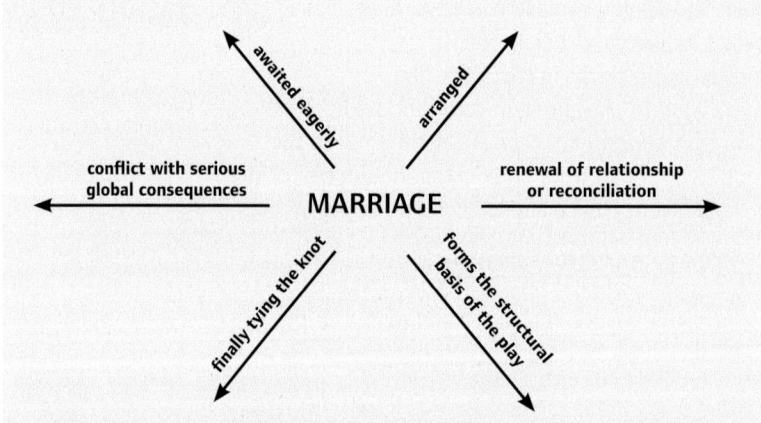

b Explain why Shakespeare might have chosen to present so many aspects of love and marriage in the play.

C2 The structure of the play

Read the info box below and complete task 1 on the next page.

> **Info Dramatic structure**
> Elizabethan playwrights followed classical dramatic theory and divided plays into five distinctive sections. Modern dramas do not follow this structure anymore, but in Shakespeare's plays, it is still relevant in order to understand the pattern of the plot.

5 The action begins with the **introduction** or **exposition**, which presents the protagonists and the main plot, and is then driven forward by the **inciting moment**, i.e. an event which leads to a conflict or problem that needs to be solved during the play. Further conflicts complicate the plot, and the characters meet more obstacles in the next phase. This is the **rising action**. Often, there are sub-plots mirroring the theme or action of the main plot, which are usually resolved before the ending of the main action. The highest point of
10 tension is reached with the **climax** or **turning-point**, which marks a complete change for the protagonist(s). It can either be a change for the better (in a comedy) or for the worse (in a tragedy). Next comes the **falling action**, which is usually shorter than the rising action, and contains developments leading to the **resolution** (in a comedy) or the **catastrophe** (in a tragedy) that ends the play. In comedies, the characters are reconciled
15 and marriages are likely, whereas the hero of a tragedy dies.

1 Illustrate where the main elements of drama (bold letters in the text above) can be found in *A Midsummer Night's Dream*. Which plots would you call sub-plots and what functions do the first and the last scenes of the play serve?

C3 *A Midsummer Night's Dream* 3.0

1 `Writing` Imagine a text message conversation between characters that is not part of the play, e.g. Puck telling a fairy about his actions during the night, Oberon demanding the changeling boy from Titania while she is under his magic spell, or Titania arguing with Oberon whether it is right not to have given Demetrius the antidote to the love juice. Write their conversation.

2 Design a meme or GIF for the whole play and collect your creations using an online presentation tool.

3 `Writing` Using an online tool, create a fake social-media profile and status for a character of your choice. Write his or her posts and add photos, links and video clips they might want to share.

4 `Writing` Write a text which is not part of the comedy, e.g. Lysander's love letters to Hermia or the ballad of Bottom's dream.

5 `Writing` Rewrite the narration of a past event in the play in another text format, like a song, a poem or a cartoon. You can pick from events such as the fairy couple's accusations of adultery, Titania's report on the seasons' changes and the changeling boy's mother, Oberon's memory of Cupid's actions in Act II, Scene 1 or Helena's recollection of her and Hermia's friendship in Act III, Scene 2.

6 Transform the quotes from the play on the next page into emoji characters/emoticons and, as a class/group, decide who had the best solution.

> Egeus: 'Full of vexation come I, with complaint against my child, my daughter Hermia.' (Act I, Scene 1, ll. 22-23)

> Oberon: 'Wake when some vile thing is near.' (Act II, Scene 2, l. 34)

> Puck: 'Lord, what fools these mortals be!' (Act III, Scene 2, l. 115)

7 a Writing In small groups, write a newspaper edition covering the events of Act V in different types of articles, e.g. breaking news, a court circular, human interest story, interview, letters to the editor, review or advertisement. Each group chooses a different type of article.

b Once every group is finished with their article, gather them to create a small newspaper entirely devoted to Act V of *A Midsummer Night's Dream*.

8 Create an illustrated one-page response with words and images which expresses how you engaged with either the ideas or themes of the play, a scene, a line or the play's title.

9 a Find a brief character description of Orsino and use it to describe the cartoon on the right.

b Imagine characters from *A Midsummer Night's Dream* are using the internet in different ways. Find activities for the prankster Puck, the ham actor Bottom and another character of your choice.

10 a Create a video trailer for a new version of the play. Decide on an angle for the plot (e.g. a fantasy story or a love story), write a narration and choose key scenes without giving away the ending.

b Speaking Present your trailer to the class. Explain the stylistic choices you made.

11 a Go online and find modern music for two dances in the play: the fairy couple's dance (Act IV, Scene 1, 83–84) and the Mechanicals' Bergomask (Act V, Scene 1, 337–338).

b Speaking Present your music selection to the class and justify your choices.

12 a Examine how Lysander's remark 'The course of true love never did run smooth' (Act I, Scene 1, l. 134) fits each of the play's couples.

b Compare the couples' struggles to the way love is shown in modern romantic comedies.

SHAKESPEAREAN CHARACTERS ON THE INTERNET

©2022 Mya Lixian Gosling - goodticklebrain.com

Info Bergamask
In the play *A Midsummer Night's Dream*, a rustic dance from the Italian region of Bergamo is mentioned: the **bergomask**. Although the spelling with an 'o' is used in the play, it is also commonly written with an 'a': bergamask.

The Founder

Part A
Pre-viewing activities

A1 Working with a film poster

1 a **Think:** Go online and look for posters of the film *The Founder*.
   b **Pair:** With a partner, make predictions as to what the film could be about. Consider the film's title on the poster, the image, the colours, the font used for the texts, etc.
   c **Share:** Share your ideas in class.

A2 Talking about fast food restaurants

1 a Make a list of five fast food restaurants that you consider the most important in your area.
   b Share your list with your class. Then, as a class, have a vote. Rank the top five winners from 1–5.
2 Work in pairs. Discuss what you know about fast food restaurants. What do different fast food restaurants have in common? What do people like/dislike about them? Why do some people go to fast food restaurants and others don't?

Part B
While-viewing activities

B1 'The most remarkable restaurant'

Making predictions

1 The beginning of the film *The Founder* is set in 1954. As a class, imagine what fast food restaurants looked like at that time.

Comprehension

2 Viewing Watch the opening segment of the film (0:00:00–00:15:49) and complete the following sentences.

A Ray Kroc works as a _____.

B In the drive-in restaurants where he eats, he encounters two problems:

_____ and _____.

C While listening to a motivational speech in his hotel room, Ray notes that the most

important key word is _____.

D When Ray hears from his secretary that six milkshake mixers have been ordered, he thinks

that _____.

E The mixers were ordered by a restaurant called _____ in

_____, _____ (city and state).

F When he first ordered a burger at this restaurant, two things surprised Ray:

_____ and

_____.

G Three principles are key to the restaurant: 1) _____;

2) _____; 3) _____.

126

Analysis

3 Writing Write a short text in which you characterize Ray as he has been presented so far. Refer to specific scenes to support your analysis (→ Info box, p. 152).

Language help

| successful – unsuccessful | ambitious – lazy | impressed – unimpressed |
| honest – dishonest | driven – indifferent | |

Beyond the text

4 a Go online and research the concept of the assembly line. Collect the information in the second column of the table below:

	assembly line	McDonald's restaurant
year of invention		(information not given yet)
inventor		
purpose		
main principles		

b Compare the process of making a burger at Dick and Mac's restaurant with that of an assembly line. Fill in the third column of the table with your observations.

5 a Consider the advantages and disadvantages of this kind of production process for business owners, workers, and consumers. With a partner, plan a two-minute radio interview in which one of you is the host and the other is an assembly line expert.

b Speaking Perform your interview in front of the class.

B2 'So that's our story'

Making predictions

1 a Work with a partner. Note down what steps need to be taken when starting a business.

b Compare your results in class. Add further items to your list if needed.

c Speculate how the business of the McDonald brothers may have started.

Comprehension

2 a `Viewing` In the next short segment of the film (00:15:50–00:24:10), the McDonald brothers explain to Ray Kroc how they developed their business idea. As you watch this segment, note down what problems the brothers encounter and how they solve them. Collect your results in the table below:

	Problem(s)	Solution(s)
the beginning		
the first business		
the second business: – location – costs – moving the stand		
drive-in restaurants: – clients – costs – waiting time		
opening day		
reopening night		

b Explain why Dick and Mac didn't give up after the problems that occurred on their opening night? Write 2-3 sentences.

Analysis

3 a Work in pairs. Compare your list of the steps from 1a/b with the story of the McDonald brothers. Note down where you find similarities and where there are aspects that differ.

b Compare the development of the McDonald's business with your predictions from 1c.

c `Writing` Write a comment on Dick's following statement: 'It's a symphony of efficiency.' Is it a suitable description of the segment

you just watched? Consider how Dick and Mac McDonald developed the concept for their kitchen.

Beyond the text

4 a Read the definition of the American Dream
(→ Info box) and take notes on how this notion is
reflected in the story of the McDonald brothers. Are
they living the American Dream?

b Prepare a short speech in which you present your
arguments from **a**. Make sure your speech includes:
– an introduction which contains an interesting
opening and a definition of the American Dream,
– a main part in which you develop your argument,
– a conclusion in which you summarize your
message and end with an outlook.

c **Speaking** Get together in groups of three and present your
speeches to each other.

Info The American Dream

The American Dream is a set of beliefs central to the self-conception of the USA. Based
on the words from the Declaration of Independence that 'all men are created equal', it
contains the idea that every person in the USA can gain economic success if they work
hard, no matter what social class they are born into. In the 19th century, the USA presented
itself as the land of unlimited opportunity, especially with settlements reaching the West
Coast and seemingly unlimited lands stretched before anyone who was willing to travel west
and find their luck.

B3 'The new American church'

Making predictions

1 As a class, discuss what you think Ray Kroc is going to do next.

Comprehension

2 **Viewing** Watch the next segment of the film (00:24:11–00:56:44)
and complete the following sentences by ticking the correct answer.

a After hearing the story of the creation of the McDonald's
restaurant, Ray Kroc wants to …

    A buy the business.
    B buy a lot of McDonald's stocks.
    C invest in the business and become a partner.
    D convince the brothers to franchise their business.

b The brothers see a problem with franchising because …

    A it's too expensive.
    B they have not tried it before.
    C they cannot control the products' quality well enough.
    D they cannot find people who want to supervise the restaurants.

c The 'Golden Arches' were designed by …

    A Ray Kroc.
    B Dick McDonald.
    C the McDonald brothers.
    D the person who runs the Phoenix restaurant.

d Before he discovered the McDonald's restaurant, Ray Kroc …

    A had gone to business school.
    B had been a successful salesman.
    C had been an unsuccessful salesman.
    D had tried different business ideas with varying success.

e When the banker asks Ray about the golden arches, he …

    A claims they are his own idea.
    B completely ignores the question.
    C credits Dick McDonald with the idea.
    D answers the question without saying whose idea it was.

f In order to raise money to build his first restaurants, Ray …

    A sells his house.
    B sells stocks and bonds.
    C takes out a business loan.
    D takes out a new mortgage on his house.

g The construction of Ray's first restaurant is slowed down because …

    A the basement has caved in.
    B the builders are working too slowly.
    C the builders have not put in the correct heating system.
    D the brothers have concerns about the safety of the building.

h For his first restaurant, Ray wants the Coca Cola company to ...

    A pay for the front window.
    B sponsor the menu boards.
    C be the sole provider of drinks.
    D determine the colour of the menu boards.

i When Ray presents his idea at the club, his wife ...

    A supports him.
    B tries to stop him.
    C adds interesting information.
    D ignores his attempt to win investors.

j Ray is angry because the other club members who opened a franchise ...

    A cannot cook.
    B do not work in their restaurants themselves.
    C are not successful enough with their restaurants.
    D serve food that is not normally served at McDonald's restaurants.

Analysis

3 a Viewing Re-watch the segment in which Ray tries to convince the McDonald brothers of starting a larger franchising concept (00:32:28–00:34:40). Note down the gist of his arguments. Take specific notes on the institutions, the symbols and the values that Ray mentions.

b Viewing Watch the entire segment again (00:24:11–00:56:44). Take note of the passages in which Ray's idea of business ethics differs from that of the McDonald brothers. Collect your results in the table below:

Ray Kroc	the McDonald brothers

c Viewing Watch the last part of this segment again (00:50:50–
00:56:44). Take notes on the following questions:
- How are Leonard Rosenblatt and his wife different than the
  other club members as franchisees?
- What key concepts does Ray use to sell the idea of McDonald's
  restaurants to potential franchisees?

4 Writing The concept behind McDonald's that Ray Kroc describes to
the McDonald brothers differs from that which he presents to future
franchisees. Write an interior monologue (→ Info box, p. 36) from
Ray's perspective in which he debates and decides what to say to
everyone involved.

Beyond the text

5 a With a partner, discuss how the following characters shown in
this segment exemplify certain aspects of the American Dream
(→ Info box, p. 129).

Ray Kroc	Ethel Kroc	The McDonald brothers	Leonard Rosenblatt and his wife	other franchisees

b Examine the role the American Dream plays in Ray Kroc's concept
for selling the idea of McDonald's.

B4 'The nerve of this guy'

Making predictions

1 a Evaluate which of the two parties – the McDonald brothers
or Ray Kroc – deserve more credit for the growth of the
McDonald's restaurants. Consider the following aspects:
- original ideas
- ambition
- hard work
- expansion of the ideas

b Discuss your ideas with a partner, then share your results in class.

Comprehension

2 Viewing Watch the next segment of the film (00:56:45–01:14:05)
and complete the following sentences using information from the
film segment.

A Dick and Mac McDonald are upset because Ray Kroc has called his Des Plaines

restaurant '_____.'

B Fred Turner (who was flipping burgers in Ray's first restaurant) is now his

_____.

C When asked when he started McDonald's, Ray answers: '_____

_____.' (Write the exact words.)

D The percentage that Ray gets from the restaurants' revenue is _____%.

E Ray calls the brothers and says he wants to _____,

asking for _____.

F Ethel is angry because Ray has _____.

G Joan Smith comes up with the idea to save electrical costs by using _____

_____.

H When Ray says he'll think about Joan's idea, Rollie Smith says:

'_____.' (Write the exact words.)

I Ray cannot put Joan's idea into action because _____

_____.

Analysis

3 Consider once more the answers you noted down in sentences **A**, **C**, and **H** from **2**. Write a short text analysing the context in which these words are spoken in the film and what they mean. Watch out for subtle hints (hesitations, looks, etc.).

B5 'The concept of winning'

Making predictions

1 From what you have observed in the film so far, take notes on what you think will happen to the following:
  - the further development of the McDonald's company
  - Ray Kroc's personal life
  - his relationship to the McDonald brothers

Comprehension

2 a `Viewing` Watch the final segment of the film (01:14:05–01:44:45). Form seven groups in your class, each of which gets a separate viewing task:

Group 1:
Note down the steps in which Ray Kroc develops and expands the McDonald's enterprise. Use a blue note card or a blue pen on a white note card.

Group 2:
Note down details of how Ray deals with the McDonald brothers as well as the contract he has signed with them. Use a red note card or a red pen on a white note card.

Group 3:
Note down details that outline Ray's relationships with both Ethel and Joan. Use a yellow note card or a yellow pen on a white note card.

Group 4:
Note down details that show reasons why Ray came out as the winner. Use a pink note card or a pink pen on a white note card.

Group 5:
At the end, Ray hands out a business card with the word 'FOUNDER' printed in capital letters on it. Note down scenes and quotations that indicate who the real founder(s) of McDonald's is/are. Use a green note card or a green pen on a white note card.

Group 6:
Note down information that helps you outline Ray's character. Use a purple note card or a purple pen on a white note card.

Group 7:
Note down information that helps you outline the characters of Dick and Mac McDonald. Use an orange note card or an orange pen on a white note card.

b Exchange your results in class. Arrange your note cards on a pin board to form a collage of the main themes of the story.

Analysis

3 a In your groups from **2**, think back on the earlier segments of the film and note down scenes that have hinted at the outcomes in the final segment. Use white notecards and a black or blue pen.

b Present your results in class, adding your notecards to the collage to form a comprehensive summary of the film.

Beyond the text

4 a Writing Put yourself into the position of one of the following characters (**A**, **B** or **C**) and write a letter from their perspective.

A Ethel: After the divorce, you write a letter to Ray in which you reflect on your relationship from the time of his early business ventures to the divorce settlement.

B Joan: After Ray's death in 1984, you write a letter to your former husband Rollie in which you explain your choices.

C Mac McDonald: After your restaurant sign has been taken down, you write a letter to your brother Dick in which you reflect on your roles in the development of the business.

b Present your letters to the class. While listening to your classmates' letters, observe whether the thoughts expressed, the tone and the content of the letters fit with the way the characters are presented in the film.

5 When openly admitting to breaching his contract, Ray says to the McDonald brothers:

> 'Business is war. Dog eat dog, rat eat rat. If my competitor was drowning, I'd walk right over there and stuff a hose into his mouth.'

a Discuss this statement in class. Consider the following aspects:
  – What is the message of the statement?
  – How is it reflected in the film?
  – How does it make the different people in the film feel?

b Comment on whether Ray Kroc's procedures are ethical.

c Contrast the brothers' sense of business ethics with Ray's statement. How could you formulate their credo?

6 Work on either **a** or **b**.

a Writing Write a comment on what was needed to make the McDonald's restaurants what they are today.

b Writing Write a comment on who is right, who is wrong and who was wronged in this story.

7 Discuss whether or not Ray Kroc has lived the American Dream (→ Info box, p. 129).

Part C
Post-viewing activities

C1 Working with a film review

Before you read

1 a At the end of **C1**, you are going to write a review of the film *The Founder*. Begin by making a list of the aspects you liked or did not like about the film. Collect your ideas in the table below.

Likes	Dislikes

b If you were to make a film about McDonald's restaurants, what topics would you focus on? What aspects would you add that are not covered in *The Founder*? Which aspects would you omit? Take notes.

Comprehension

2 Read the review of the film *The Founder* that appeared in *The Guardian* on the following page. Match the following headings to the paragraphs from the article they could be matched to. Write the number of the paragraph in the table below. There is one more heading than you need.

Heading	Paragraph
A Themes of the movie	
B Persistence	
C Ray's self-images	
D The film in a nutshell	
E The beginning	
F Regrets	
G The vision	
H Tricks in business	
I The appearance of Ray Kroc	
J The allure of McDonald's restaurants	

Michael Keaton supersizes McDonald's and births Trump's US

Peter Bradshaw

(1) All this film's irony and ambiguity are showcased in the title, though Birth of a Salesman was an alternative that occurred to me. *The Founder* is an absorbing and unexpectedly subtle movie about the genesis of the McDonald's burger empire. There is an avoiding of
5 obviousness that resides in its clever casting of not-immediately-dislikable Michael Keaton as Ray Kroc, the needy, driven, insecure marketing type with the predatory surname who masterminded a nationwide franchising for the original California hamburger restaurant in the 1950s; finally taking it away from its owners and revolutionary
10 fast-food pioneers, Dick and Mac McDonald, played by Nick Offerman and John Carroll Lynch.

(2) Keaton is never the cartoon bad guy, not even at the very end. His moonfaced openness makes him look like a giant, middle-aged baby, wide-eyed with optimism about the world. He looks like the kind of
15 unemployed comedian who might earn a buck playing scary clown Ronald McDonald – who is not in fact mentioned in the film.

(3) The film's first act is careful to show Kroc sympathetically; screenwriter Robert D Siegel and director John Lee Hancock cleverly set up Ray's early struggle, his genuine ecstasy on discovering the McDonald
20 brothers and his acumen in seeing the global potential of their little burger joint. And is it so wrong to call him the Founder? After all, the corporate-franchised experience of going into McDonald's anywhere in the world is what Kroc envisioned and effectively founded. Along the way, the film shows us something about postwar entrepreneurial
25 capitalism, innovation, corporate expansion and intellectual property rights. It even casts an oblique light on the new age of Trump.

(4) Keaton's Kroc is a hardworking man who's always on the road, driving from town to town, exasperated by slow and erratic service at the drive-ins where he gets lunch, while his bored wife (a thankless role
30 for Laura Dern) stays at home. Ray is trying to sell restaurant managers a new five-spindled milkshake machine – which makes five times as much as the usual single-spindle model – and crucially sell them on the concept that an increase in supply creates its own demand through market stimulus. The poor guy gets doors slammed in his face all over
35 the country. But not in California, where a couple of bright, cheery brothers, Dick and Mac McDonald, have created an extraordinarily efficient fast-food system in their burger restaurant with no plates, no cutlery, no tedious wait times. They want six or eight of Kroc's five-spindle milkshake machines. They don't have to create demand. They've
40 already got more than they can handle.

1 ambiguity [ˌæmbɪˈɡjuːəti]: uncertainty, unclarity
showcase sth.: present sth.
3 absorbing (adj): entertaining, capturing of one's attention
3 subtle [ˈsʌtl]: (here) clever, not immediately noticeable
4 genesis [ˈdʒenəsɪs]: beginning
7 predatory: hunting without a conscience, (here) greedy,
20 acumen [ˈækjəmən]: ability to see sth. and react smartly
24 entrepreneurial [ˌɒntrəprəˈnɜːriəl]: related to business and making money, ambitious
26 oblique [əˈbliːk] (adj): indirect
28 exasperated: very annoyed
34 market stimulus [ˈstɪmjələs]: monetary policy aimed at helping an economic sector grow
38 tedious [ˈtiːdiəs]: boring and taking a long time

(5) Ray listens to their story and is electrified by their innovative genius and American can-do. He positively insists on setting up a franchise operation for them. Too late, the poor McDonald brothers realise that this pushy fellow has pulled off what might be America's
45 first corporate takeover.

(6) Like the young Donald Trump, Kroc is a huge fan of self-help and how-to-win-friends-and-influence-people type stuff. Alone in his scuzzy hotel rooms, he listens to a motivational LP which intones the words of Calvin Coolidge: 'Nothing in the world can take the place of
50 persistence, talent will not, nothing is more common than unsuccessful men with talent …' It was the McDonald brothers who had the talent. Kroc was the one with the persistence. Yet that, after all, is a kind of talent.

(7) Also like Trump, Kroc's wealth is to be founded on land and real
55 estate, not burgers. He finally understands the importance of buying the land for his franchise outlets. And like Trump, he becomes an early connoisseur of branding and market identity. To the brothers' astonishment, he takes out a copyright on their solidly reassuring name. And he finally returns to his supply-over-demand theory: America
60 didn't know it wanted or needed an identikit burger joint until he gave it to them.

(8) Yet for all this, *The Founder* has a very different effect to, say, Morgan Spurlock's gonzo documentary *Super Size Me* from 2004, which set out to show America's Big Mac habit as nasty and damaging. However
65 bad Kroc's behaviour in this film, and however poignant the innocence of poor Mac and Dick, the actual customers of the restaurant are never shown as anything other than happy. Perhaps we are invited to see all this as the inevitable, rough business of market forces.

(9) Crucially, Keaton's Ray does not see himself as a sociopath or a
70 narcissist but as the Capraesque hero of a feelgood underdog drama. He thinks he is the little guy making good. Yet by the end, we have seen quite another side to him.

From: Bradshaw, Peter. 'The Founder review: Michael Keaton supersizes McDonald's and births Trump's US'. theguardian.com, 16.01.2017.

45 corporate takeover: purchase of a company by another company
48 scuzzy ['skʌzi] (infml, AE): not pleasant, disgusting
57 connoisseur [ˌkɒnəˈsɜː(r)]: person who knows a lot about a specific topic
57 branding: process of giving a product or company a distinct and recognizable name, design, symbol, etc
58 reassuring (adj): giving a feeling of security and comfort
60 identikit (adj, BE): similar to sth. else in an unoriginal way, copied
63 gonzo = gonzo journalism (infml, AE): style of reporting that aims at shocking people
65 poignant ['pɔɪnjənt]: moving, creating strong feelings of sadness
69 sociopath: mentally ill person who behaves in an unacceptable or dangerous way towards others
70 Capraesque: referring to Frank Capra (1897– 1991), a movie maker who stressed the positive aspects of courageous characters

Analysis

3 Read the text again. Identify which of the following elements of a movie review can be found in which paragraph of the text. Fill in the table on the next page. Certain elements need to be used more than once.

evaluation of the film

summary

description of main characters

main themes of the film

analysis of individual parts

Paragraph	Element of a movie review
1	
2	
3	
4	
5	
6	
7	
8	
9	

Beyond the text

4 a Go back to your own notes from **1**. Mark the ones that are similar to the review, those that are different, as well as the aspects you have added.

b `Writing` Write your own film review (→ Info box, p. 154). Use the notes you collected from **1** and **4a**.

c `Speaking` Present your texts in class.

d While listening to your classmates' reviews, take notes on how well they have included the elements of a film review, and how clearly they have expressed and illustrated their views. Give each other feedback.

139

Boy Erased

Part A
Pre-viewing activities

A1 Getting started

1 **a** **Think:** Look at the license plate above. What do you expect from life in a 'land of opportunity'?
   b **Pair:** Discuss your ideas with a partner.
   c **Share:** With another pair, discuss your ideas and decide on the two most important ones.

A2 Making predictions

1 **a** Look for film posters of *Boy Erased* online. Choose the one that appeals to you the most and examine the person/people, its colours and shading, and the depiction of the title.
   b With a partner, talk about what you expect from the film based on the poster you have chosen in **a**.
2 **a** Watch the trailer of the film online.
   b Discuss how the trailer meets your predictions from **1b**.

Part B
While-viewing activities

B1 Setting the scene

Comprehension

1 | Viewing | Watch the exposition (→ Info box) of *Boy Erased*
(00:00:00–00:11:04). Pay attention to the following aspects.

| places | people | action | dominant colours | music / sounds |

> **Info The exposition of a film**
> In films, as in dramas, the opening sequence contains important information.
> The viewers are introduced to the setting, to the main characters and their relationships,
> to previous events that determine the plot of the film, and often also to the central
> conflict that the film will be dealing with. This opening sequence is called the exposition.

Analysis

2 **a** Analyse the atmosphere of the exposition.
  b Discuss whether the atmosphere confirms your predictions
    from **A2** (p. 140).
3 Speculate on the aims of the 'Refuge Programme'.
4 State the central conflict.

Beyond the text

5 **a** Research 'conversion therapy' in the USA.
    Find out about the following aspects.

| methods | consequences | laws | advocates | legal status in different US states |

  b Get together in groups of 3-4 and exchange the results of your
    findings.
6 | WRITING | Your English class is working on a joint project on the
topic of diversity with a class from a US high school. A website with
information on different diversity topics will be created specifically for
the project. Write a blog entry on 'conversion therapy' for the
website.

B2 Conversion therapy

1 `Mediation` While working on the joint project with the US high
school (**B1, 6,** p. 141), your US team partner has come across a
German article on the topic of 'conversion therapy'. They don't
understand the article completely. Write them an email in which you
summarize the most important aspects of the article.

„Allein das Signal eines Verbots ist enorm wichtig" *Parvin Sadigh*

Therapien, die Homosexuelle vorgeblich heilen, sollen verboten werden.
Gut so, sagt die Psychiaterin Lieselotte Mahler. Menschen können ihr
Leben lang darunter leiden.

[...] Lieselotte Mahler ist Oberärztin an der Klinik für Psychiatrie und
5 Psychotherapie an der Charité in Berlin und leitet das DGPPN-Referat
für sexuelle Orientierung und Identität. Sie beschäftigt sich damit,
welche Folgen es für Menschen haben kann, wenn sie sich derart
therapieren lassen.

ZEIT ONLINE: Wie findet man heraus, ob etwa ein Arzt oder eine
10 Psychotherapeutin eine sogenannte Konversionstherapie anbietet, also
eine Therapie um Homosexuelle „zu heilen"?

Lieselotte Mahler: Das ist gar nicht so leicht. Es gibt explizite
Konversionsangebote – und zwar nicht nur von Medizinern und
Psychotherapeuten, sondern auch von Priestern, Seelsorgern oder von
15 selbsternannten Coaches. Doch die werben in der Regel nicht damit.
Menschen, die Hilfe suchen, googeln auch nicht unbedingt nach diesem
Wort. Trotzdem finden sie schnell, was sie suchen – oft im kirchlichen
Rahmen. Beim Bund katholischer Ärzte beschäftigt sich eine
Arbeitsgruppe damit. Viele evangelikale Kirchen vermitteln die
20 sogenannten Therapien.

Darüber hinaus gibt es Patienten, die eine Psychotherapie aus anderen
Gründen aufsuchen. Und währenddessen fragt der Therapeut dann
etwa: Könnte ihr Problem nicht an ihrer sexuellen Orientierung liegen?
Auf diese Weise geraten sie in eine Konversionstherapie hinein.

25 **ZEIT ONLINE:** Was geschieht in so einer Therapie?

Mahler: Manchmal wird gesellschaftlich erwartetes Verhalten
eintrainiert. Also Männer sollen sich männliche Hobbys suchen, Frauen
sich besonders weiblich kleiden. Denn dahinter steckt die Überzeugung:
Wer sich männlich verhält, kann auch nicht schwul sein oder wer sich
30 typisch weiblich verhält, nicht lesbisch.

ZEIT ONLINE: Sind es immer religiöse Menschen, die so eine Therapie
freiwillig aufsuchen oder hineingedrängt werden?

Mahler: Viele junge Menschen hadern zunächst mit ihrer sexuellen Orientierung, wenn sie merken, dass sie anders sind als die Mehrheit.
35 Minderheitenstress nennen wir das. Sie haben große Angst vor Mobbing, Diskriminierung und Gewalt. Allerdings suchen sich Menschen, die aus einem sehr religiösen Umfeld kommen, besonders häufig Hilfe bei sogenannten Homoheilern. Sie haben vielleicht explizit in der Gemeinde gehört, dass ihre sexuelle Orientierung eine Sünde ist. Sie fürchten
40 stärker als andere, dass Familie und Freunde sich von ihnen abwenden. Und sie geraten auch in Widerspruch mit den eigenen Vorstellungen von einem sinnvollen Leben, das sie sich nur als Zusammenleben von Mann und Frau vorstellen können. Es handelt sich dann um eine internalisierte Homophobie, um die Überzeugung: Ich bin abartig. [...]

45 **ZEIT ONLINE:** Können Sie beschreiben, welche Folgen eine solche Behandlung für die betroffenen Menschen hat?

Mahler: Es suchen sich ja ohnehin nur die Menschen Hilfe, die mit ihrer Homosexualität hadern: die etwa Angst vor Diskriminierung haben und sich selbst abwerten. Das allein führt schon zu hohem Stress und erhöht die Wahrscheinlichkeit, etwa eine Angsterkrankung zu entwickeln. Sie
50 bräuchten also Unterstützung für ihr Selbstwertgefühl. Stattdessen befeuert ein Arzt oder Seelsorger mit einer Konversionstherapie ihren Stress, indem er behauptet, eine sexuelle Orientierung sei heilbar. Aber Homosexualität ist keine Krankheit, und sie kann auch nicht durch äußere Intervention verändert werden. Also steht am Ende die Überzeugung: Ich scheitere, ich bin nicht stark genug, mein sündiges
55 Verhalten zu verändern. Die betroffenen Menschen sehen die Schuld bei sich selbst. Das kann zu massiven Selbstwertstörungen bis hin zur Depression und Suizidalität führen.

ZEIT ONLINE: Halten Sie das geplante Verbot der Konversionstherapien also für sinnvoll und durchsetzbar?

60 **Mahler:** Sinnvoll auf jeden Fall. Gerade wenn Kinder und Jugendliche so etwas erleben, ist die Gefahr besonders hoch, dass sie ein Leben lang unter den Folgen solcher Interventionen leiden werden. Dass sie etwa nachhaltig Schwierigkeiten haben, Beziehungen zu führen. Wie ein solches Gesetz durchsetzbar ist, überlasse ich den Juristen. Natürlich
65 rechnen Therapeuten und Ärzte offiziell schon jetzt nie eine Konversionstherapie bei den Krankenkassen ab und viele Patienten schämen sich zu sehr, um sie anzuzeigen. Ich glaube aber, Alkohol am Steuer zu verbieten war auch sinnvoll, selbst wenn man nicht jeden erwischen wird, der betrunken fährt.

70 Allein das Signal ist enorm wichtig. Deutlich zu sagen: Solche Behandlungen sind verboten, weil sie Menschen schädigen. Viele schwule und lesbische Jugendliche haben Angst vor ihrem Outing.

Wenn sie danach googeln, kann ein solches Verbot zu einem wichtigen protektiven Aspekt werden. Es wird ihnen klar: Ich bin nicht krank, ich
75 brauche keine Heilung, sondern Unterstützung. [...]

Von: „Allein das Signal eines Verbots ist enorm wichtig", Zeit Online, 11. Juni 2019.

B3 Jared's story: The beginning

Comprehension

1 a **Viewing** Watch the film from 00:11:05–00:54:16. While watching, pay attention to the following characters and fill in the table.

Name	Relation to Jared	Behaviour / Character traits
Marshall		
Nancy		
Chloe		
family doctor		
Henry		
Victor		
Michael		
Jon		

b Compare your results with a partner and add information to your table if necessary.

2 a Put the following events of Jared's story in chronological order using the timeline below and on the next page.

An anonymous caller tells Nancy and Marshall about their son's sexual inclinations.

Marshall wants the doctor to check Jared's testosterone level.

Chloe and Jared kiss in the car.

creating genograms

exercise on masculinity

Henry rapes Jared.

Sarah's moral inventory

Nancy tells Jared about his gay uncle.

Jared's resolution to change in a conversion therapy

A

↓

B

↓

C

↓

D

↓

E

↓

F

↓

G

H

I

b Describe how Jared's story is told and explain the reasons for this technique.

Analysis

3 `Viewing` In small groups, watch the following scenes again.
Group 1: 00:15:11–00:17:53
Group 2: 00:31:44–00:34:14
Group 3: 00:49:55–00:52:20

a Make notes on how the dominant character in your scene influences Jared and his future.

b Discuss your ideas with the other members of your group.

4 a Prepare a tableau (→ Info box) showing the relationship between Jared and your chosen character. Take a picture.

b Present the picture of your tableau to the class and let them describe and analyse it. Be prepared to explain or make additions.

Info Tableau

A tableau is a living sculpture which depicts different characters in a typical pose or gesture, expressing their mood with a frozen facial expression. It is advisable to choose one or two group members as directors who move the characters, show them where and how to stand, and advise them on what body language to use before the members in character 'freeze'. Taking a picture of the tableau once it is set makes it easier to show to the class and let them analyse it.

Beyond the text

5 Viewing Watch 00:52:21–00:54:16.
  a Sum up what the doctor says to Jared.
  b Compare her opinion with that of Jared's parents.
  c Assess the influence the doctor has on Jared.
  d Writing After Jared has seen his doctor, he is confused and does not know what to think and do. Write his interior monologue (→ Info box, p. 36).

B4 Jared's story: The development

Comprehension

1 Viewing Watch the film from 00:54:17–01:34:53.
Summarize what happens in the following segments by completing sentences **A–K** below.

First doubts (00:54:17–01:03:05)
A Victor advises Jared to _____

_____.

B When presenting the results of his moral inventory to the group, Gary _____

_____.

C While Nancy is reading Jared's confession, he talks to her about _____

_____.

Xavier (01:03:06–01:07:01 and 01:19:59–01:21:26)
D Jared and Xavier meet at _____.

E The evening leads to _____.

_____.

Growing uncertainty (01:07:02–01:16:08)
F When Jared is left behind with Cameron, he tries to comfort him by _____

_____.

G In the restroom, Brandon _____

_____.

147

H Over the phone, Jared tells his father _____

_____ .

Cameron (01:16:09–01:34:53)

I In the presence of his family, Cameron has to take part in _____

_____ .

J He is also beaten up in order to _____ .

K A few days later, Cameron _____ .

Analysis

2 Viewing Watch 01:22:22–01:25:50 again.

   a Examine Victor Sykes's way of questioning Jared.

   b Explain Jared's reaction to Victor's method.

3 Watch the following scenes again and analyse how the different characters behave in the programme as well as how they cope with the situation they are in.

Jon (00:18:40–00:20:29)

Gary (01:12:15–01:14:04)

Cameron (01:21:25–01:22:22)

4 a Together with a partner, examine Jared's behaviour in the programme and his development while coping with the situation. Assess who and what influences Jared's development.

   b Visualize your results.

Beyond the text

5 Choose **a** or **b**.

   a Writing After Nancy has picked up Jared from the therapy center, she writes a letter of complaint to the board of governors in which she officially withdraws Jared from the programme. Write this letter from her perspective. Give her reasons for the withdrawal.

   b Speaking Work with a partner. After Nancy and Jared have arrived home, Nancy has a discussion with Marshall about her plans to not send Jared back to the programme. Prepare this discussion. Then act it out in front of the class.

6 **a** **Think:** If you were the director of the film, how would you let the film end? Gather ideas.

   b **Pair:** Compare your ideas with a partner. Choose one you both like and write a short draft of a possible storyline.

   c **Share:** Present your storyline to the class and discuss how realistic it is in light of what you have learned about Jared's development so far.

B5 Jared's story: The end

Comprehension

1 Viewing Watch the film from 01:34:54 until the end.

   a Answer the following questions:

   A Where does Jared live four years later?

   _____

   B What kind of relationship is he in?

   _____

   C What does he want his father to do?

   _____

   D Why is this so important for him?

   _____

   b Compare the ending with your own ideas. How accurate were your predictions?

Analysis

2 a Analyse the relationship between Nancy and Marshall as presented at the end of the film.

b Compare Nancy and Marshall's relationship at the end of the film with their relationship at the beginning. How has it evolved?

Beyond the text

3 a Research 'Baptism' and 'The Bible Belt'.

b Prepare a two-minute talk in which you explain the influence religion has on the life of the Eamons family. Use facts you learned during your research for task **a**.

c Speaking Give the talk in front of your class.

B6 The relationship between Jared and his mother

Comprehension

1 Viewing Watch the following segments again:
- 00:20:30–00:23:13
- 01:27:17–01:30:06
- 01:30:07–01:32:04

a Describe Nancy as she appears in each scene.

b Outline how Jared reacts to and behaves towards his mother.

Analysis

2 Characterize Nancy by matching adjectives from the word bank below to the three segments in task **1**.

> affectionate · assertive · brave · caring · cautious · charismatic · determined · doleful · faithful · gentle · intelligent · loving · loyal · plaintive · playful · reliable · self-confident · serious · sincere · trustworthy · wistful · witty

3 Viewing In two groups, watch the following segments again:
- Group A: 00:48:03–00:49:54
- Group B: 01:37:42–01:38:55

a Analyse Nancy's sentences from the segments by comparing what she is hinting at and what she actually means. Use the table on the next page.

What Nancy is hinting at	What Nancy means
Group A	
'Pastor Wilkes has dealt with that kind of thing before.'	
'Jim has a son...They did things for him. Just like they're gonna do things for you.'	
Group B	
'I go [to church], sometimes, I support your dad and...'	
'He knows... I can't be around the ...I love God, God loves me. And I love my son.'	

b Exchange your results with a partner from the other group.
  Fill in missing information from the other group in your table.
c With your partner, state parallels in Nancy's way of speaking.
d Explain the role Nancy takes on in her family. It might be helpful
  to visualize your ideas, either using lines and arrows or creating
  a tableau (→ Info box, p. 146).
e Characterize Nancy based on the information from your
  completed table (→ Info box, p. 152).

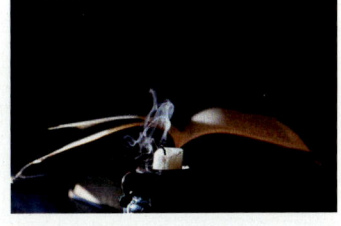

Language help
In the two extracts, Nancy is portrayed as... · The way she talks implies that ... ·
Her tone of voice can be described as ... · In conclusion, Nancy is depicted as...

Beyond the text
4 Writing At the end of the film, Jared is talking to his publishers
  regarding a book they want to publish about his story. Imagine that
  Jared dedicates his book to his mother. Write his acknowledgement
  to his mother at the end of the book, giving reasons for this decision.
5 Discuss which other people might be mentioned in the
  acknowledgements from task **4**. Briefly outline what Jared might
  write about them.

B7 The relationship between Jared and his father

Comprehension

1 **Viewing** Watch the following segments again:
  – 00:13:41–00:15:10
  – 00:44:33–00:46:52
  – 01:14:05–01:15:23
  a Outline what Marshall expects from his son.
  b Examine how Jared behaves towards his father.

2 **Viewing** Watch 01:41:50–01:47:12.
  a Outline the course of the conversation between Jared and Marshall.
  b Discuss which of the following words or expressions best describe the outcome of the conversation.

> forgiveness · reconciliation · peace · understanding · regret · acceptance · sorrow · tolerance · coming to terms

Analysis

3 **Writing** Write a character profile for Marshall (→ Info box).

> **Info Writing a characterization**
>
> **Collect all necessary information on the character:**
> personal information · appearance · family background ·
> relationship with other characters · behaviour · thoughts and attitudes
>
> **A** Start with an introduction in which you briefly introduce the character.
> **B** For the main body of the text, use paragraphs to organize your thoughts. Describe the character's outward appearance and give background information before you examine their attitudes. Use examples/quotes from the novel/film to analyse your character.
> **C** Write a conclusion to sum up your text.

4 Explain the reasons why Marshall gives Jared the pen he has always written his sermons with.
5 Analyse the development of the relationship between Jared and his father.

Beyond the text

6 **Writing** *Boy Erased* – Discuss the title of the film. Also take the German title into consideration.

B8 Coming of Age

Comprehension

1 a Viewing Re-watch the scenes given by the time codes in the table below. Make notes on stage directions that could be in the script (tone of voice, facial expression, body language). Add these notes in the second column of the table.

	Potential stage directions	How the scene is embedded
00:04:13–00:04:40		
00:58:16–00:59:35		
01:47:35–01:48:15		

b Watch the scenes a second time, starting a little earlier and ending a little later to find out how each scene is embedded in the film. Write your results in the third column of the table.

Analysis

2 Describe how Jared's behaviour changes in the three scenes from **1**.

3 Analyse the function all three scenes have for the development of the plot (→ Info box, Leitmotif).

4 Assess the importance of Jared's experiences presented in the film for the development of his identity.

Beyond the text

5 The song 'Revelation' by Troye Sivan and Jónsi serves as a leitmotif (→ Info box, Leitmotif) in the film, accompanying Jared at different stages of his coming-of-age process.

a Find the lyrics of the song on the internet.

b Outline the meaning of the lyrical attributes to the addressee.

c Examine the lyrics and illustrate the parallels to Jared's situation.

6 Writing Write a role biography (→ Info box) from Jared's point of view at the end of the film.

> **Info Leitmotif**
> A leitmotif in a film, in literature or in music is an idea, a phrase or a tune that is frequently repeated and connected with a particular character or idea.

> **Info Writing a role biography**
> When writing a role biography, you are writing about one particular character's life.
> – Put yourself in the character's shoes and use the first person perspective.
> – Write like you are writing a diary. Talk about your family and your relationship to them, your everyday life, your neighborhood, your past, and your hopes for the future; tell your reader what is important to you and what causes you problems.
> – Write the text in complete sentences.

Part C
Post- viewing activities

C1 A true story

1 *Boy Erased* is based on a novel by Garrard Conley about his life story.
  a Find out more about Conley, his career and his publications.
  b Get together with a partner and exchange your results.

A TED Talk by Garrard Conley

2 a `Viewing` Use the webcode in the right page margin to go online and watch Garrard Conley's TED Talk titled 'Embracing the mess – How compassion saved my life'.
  b Get together in groups of three. Each member of the group works on one of the three tasks below (**A**, **B** or **C**).
    While watching the Ted Talk, make notes on …
    A … parallels between Jared's and Conley's experiences.
    B … the differences between Jared's and Conley's experiences as well as on new pieces of information.
    C … thoughts and emotions Conley shares with his audience.
  c Exchange your results with the other members of your group.

Garrard Conley at The Director's Guild of America in Los Angeles on 29 October, 2018.

cornelsen.de
Code: cabayo

C2 Writing a film review

1 While finishing up the project from **B1,6**, you have been asked to write a film review of *Boy Erased* for the project's website (→ Info box).
  a Collect general information about the film as well as ideas for your review. Consider different characters and what shapes their identities (e.g. gender, family, religion, values, symbols of belonging). Focus on the characters most important to you.
  b `Writing` Write your review.

> **Info Writing a film/play review**
> In a film or play review, you provide information on a film/play you have watched and express your opinion about it. To prepare the review, make notes on interesting, positive or negative aspects you notice while watching the film/play. Collect information such as the director's name, the main actors, the running time, etc. Take note of scenes in which characters struggle to form their identity. Then structure your ideas. In the introduction of your review, give some basic information on the film/play and its questions of identity as a central theme. In the main part, briefly summarize the plot and comment on relevant aspects, especially the topic of shifting identities. Finally, give your opinion in the conclusion. State whether you recommend the film/play, potentially also recommending it for a specific target group.

seven methods of killing kylie jenner

Part A
Pre-reading activities

A1 About the author

> **Info Jasmine Lee-Jones**
> Jasmine Lee-Jones is a British actor and playwright. She was born in North London in 1998, and was only 21 years old when her first play, *seven methods of killing kylie jenner,* was put on stage in 2019. The play was highly successful and Jasmine Lee-Jones received several awards.

A2 Looking at the form of the play

1 **a** Make a list of typical features of a dramatic text.
  b Flip through the book. Note down which of the features listed in **a** can be seen. Are there further/new features?

2 a Define the term 'meme' in your own words.

b From your own experience, list typical features and functions of a meme.

3 a With a partner, flip through the book again and choose one of the memes. Together, imagine a situation in which this meme might be used.

b `Speaking` Present your idea to the class.

4 Based on what you have observed in **2** and **3**, make predictions for the play. What do you expect it will be about? Consider the title of the play in your predictions as well.

A3 Looking at the language of the play

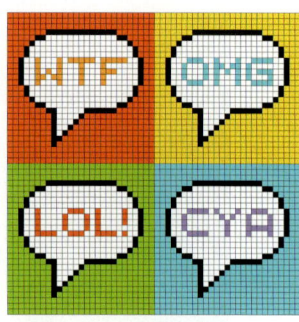

1 a With a partner, make a list of acronyms and abbreviations you use in communication on social media.

b Share your results with the class. As a class, make a list of everyone's acronyms and abbreviations.

2 a Using the webcode on the right, go online and watch a video on how to greet someone in Jamaican Creole (also known as Jamaican Patois) (→ Info box).

b Do some online research and note down more expressions in Jamaican Creole.

c Exchange your results in class.

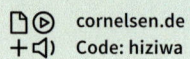

cornelsen.de
Code: hiziwa

Info Jamaican Creole

The two protagonists in *seven methods of killing kylie jenner* are Black British women. Many Black people in the UK have Jamaican or other Caribbean roots because, after World War II, people from former British colonies were encouraged to immigrate to the UK, and a large wave of immigration from the Caribbean ensued. These countries had experienced a long history of colonialization, during which indigenous languages of enslaved African people came into contact with the English of the colonizers. As a result, so-called Creole languages were formed, such as Jamaican Creole (also called **Jamaican Patois**). There are instances of Jamaican Creole in the play, for example:

– 'fi' can be used to mean futurity or obligation, like in #kyliejennerfidead, or to mean 'to', as in 'haffi' = have to.

– 'dem' is the Jamaican form of 'them' and can also be attached to a noun to give it a plural meaning.

– 'blad' stands for 'brother' or anyone who is close to you; just like 'mate' in some parts of the UK.

Part B
While-reading activities

B1 The premeditations

1 a The play begins with an introduction to its historical context in 'Premeditations I', which is said to be optional to the performance. In small groups, research one of the following terms or events mentioned in this section. Make sure each group picks a different topic.

the Corona pandemic (roadmaps and lifting lockdowns)

the Israel and Palestine conflict (around the year 2020)

the #metoo movement

bans on Black hairstyles

hate crimes against Asians

Meghan Markle and Prince Harry's interview with Oprah Winfrey

the Sarah Everard case

the 2020 US presidential election

the US Capitol riots of 6 January, 2021

Breonna Taylor and other female victims of police violence in the USA

conspiracy theories

George Floyd and the Black Lives Matter movement

the removal of statues of former slave owners

b Using the information you gathered in **a**, prepare a two-minute presentation on your topic.

c Speaking Give your presentation to the class.

2 a Read the text 'The Premeditation II' which is the real opening of the play. With a partner, discuss what you think the two women are 'burying' or concealing here.

b Exchange your ideas with your class.

B2 How it starts (Twitterlude 1, IRL)

Comprehension

1 While reading pp. 4–15, answer the following questions:

A What makes Cleo so upset that she starts tweeting about killing Kylie Jenner?

_____

B What is the idea behind the first method (#DEATHBYPOISON)?

_____

C What is the idea behind the second method (#DEATHBYSHOOTING)?

_____

D How does Cleo explain her anger to Kara in the IRL-passages?

_____

E What are the first reactions in the Twittersphere like?

_____

Kylie Jenner, reality TV/ social media star, Kim Kardashian's half-sister and owner of a successful cosmetics line, at a premiere in California in 2019.

Analysis

2 Re-read the two tweets on the first method of killing Kylie Jenner. Explain how they resemble the style of spoken word poetry (→ Info box). Give examples.

> **Info Spoken word poetry**
> 'Spoken word' is a form of poetry that is typically recited orally, for example at poetry slams. Its style is influenced by hip hop, and it often contains word play, different forms of rhyme (end rhyme, internal rhyme), alliteration and repetition.

3 Based on these initial pages of the play, examine what you have learned about the two characters and their relationship to each other?

4 Cleo's Twitter handle (@INCOGNEGRO) is a so-called portmanteau, i.e., a word that is made up of the parts of at least two words that overlap. Explain how the word is formed and what effect it has.

Beyond the text

5 With a partner, discuss whether you consider Cleo's reaction to the Forbes tweet on Kylie Jenner appropriate.

6 **Writing** Write a tweet in response to Cleo's first tweets (her direct response as well as the first two methods).

B3 **How it develops** (Twitterlude 2, IRL)

Comprehension

1 Complete the following two sentences by ticking the correct box.
   a When reacting to Cleo's tweets in the Twittersphere (pp. 17–20), people …

   A feel threatened.
   B immediately want to support her.
   C make fun of Cleo and show that they do not take her seriously.
   D question her moral values, wondering whether this is an appropriate form of social activism.

   b In the IRL (pp. 21–27), the main topic of Cleo and Kara's conversation is …

   A their friendship.
   B Cleo's recent breakup.
   C the best form of social activism.
   D the difference between Black and white women.

2 After reading pp. 16–27, summarize in your own words what happened in this section of the text.

Analysis

3 Look closely at pp. 16–27. Analyse the different functions of memes in this part of the text (e.g. the memes under 'KARA deeps shit like:' on p. 26[1]). What effect do they have on the reader?

4 Re-read Cleo's monologue on her ex-lover's new lover (p. 26). Make a list of the problematic aspects and analyse what they mean. Fill in the table on the next page to do so.

---

[1]Lee-Jones, Jasmine. *Seven methods of killing Kylie Jenner.* Methuen Drama, 2021, p. 26.

Problematic aspect	Meaning

Beyond the text

5 a When you read the play, you see the memes in context with the words that are spoken. With a partner, collect ideas for the different functions of the memes you have analysed in **3**. How could the memes be integrated into a stage performance? Prepare to perform an example for the class.

b Speaking Perform a short scene with an integrated meme for the class.

6 Writing Write a blog post in which you comment on what the use of the memes you have seen so far in the play *seven methods of killing kylie jenner* says about the influence of social media on the way we communicate.

B4 The fourth method (Twitterlude 3, IRL)

Comprehension

1 While reading pp. 28–40, fill in the gaps below to complete the summary of this passage:

In her fourth method, Cleo proposes to take off Kylie's (**A**) _____ so that she can wear it, thereby taking on Kylie's (**B**) _____ and (**C**) _____ for a short time. In the timeline, people are discussing that they want to (**D**) _____ Cleo, but in reality they

5 are staying because they are (**E**) _____ how the story will develop. In the IRL passage, Kara tries to make Cleo (**F**) _____, but Cleo turns the argument against Kara by saying that she does not understand the problem because (**G**) _____. Cleo lists a number of examples that prove that (**H**) _____

10 Black women have fewer problems than (**I**) _____ Black women, while Kara claims that (**J**) _____ share the same problems.

2 Cleo claims that Kara is in a better position because she is lighter-skinned. Kara denies this. In your notebooks, collect the arguments and examples each of the women puts forward.

Analysis

3 Re-read the tweet in which Cleo describes her fourth method. Compare what she calls 'whiteface' with the definition of 'blackface' given below (→ Info box). Where do you see similarities? What are the differences?

> **Info Blackface**
> The term blackface refers to the practice of white actors wearing dark makeup to mimic Black people. It was a regular feature of **Vaudeville shows**, a form of musical theatre that came to the USA through French immigrants and became very popular in the late 19th and early 20th century. Blackface characters often dressed in suits with top hats and performed tap dance. Features of Vaudeville shows were taken over and integrated into US **minstrel shows**, in which Black people were caricatured and ridiculed for entertainment. Today, blackface is considered deeply inappropriate and racist.

4 Refer back to the list of arguments you collected in **2**. Explain how each woman believes she is right. Is it possible that they are both right?

Beyond the text

5 `Writing` Imagine that you are Kara and you have just heard a lecture on the theory of intersectionality (→Info box). Write an email to Cleo in which you explain to her why you disagree with her claim that you have it easier in life. Include all aspects of Kara's personality that you have found out about so far.

> **Info Intersectionality**
> The concept of intersectionality describes the way in which the different social identities of a person work together to form their unique position in society. The theory of intersectionality looks at inequality based on race, gender, sexual orientation, socio-economic status, migration status, etc. It assumes that the different aspects always influence each other and cannot be looked at in isolation.
>
>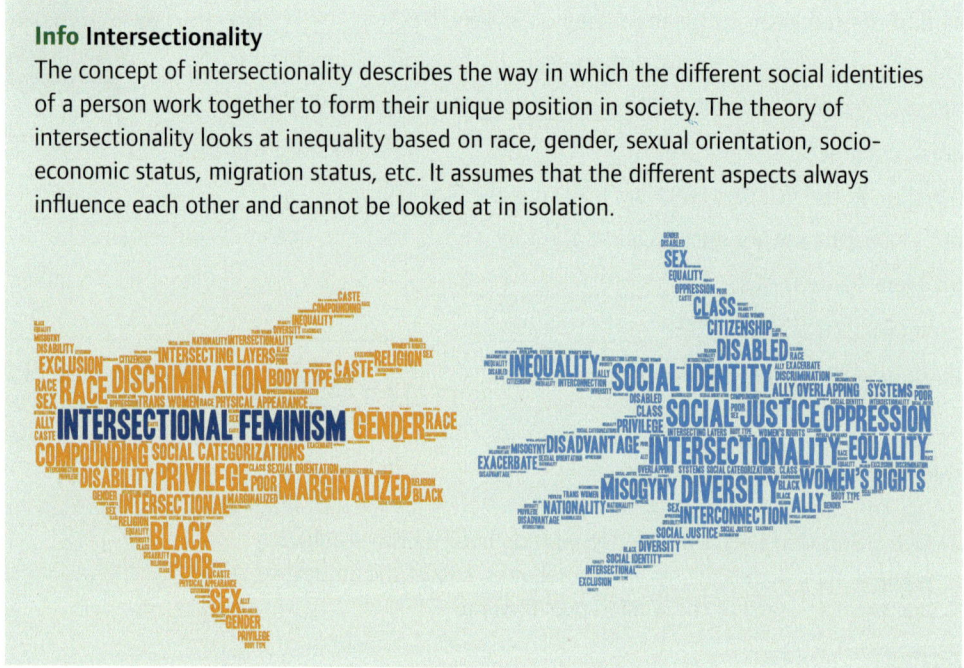

B5 Bringing up old stories (Twitterlude 4–10, IRL in between)

Comprehension

1 Read Twitterlude 4 (pp. 41–42) and fill in the following gaps:

A The fifth method of killing Kylie Jenner consists

of _____.

B The Twitter users compare Cleo to _____ and

post a picture of _____.

2 Read the IRL (pp. 43–49) and summarize in your own words what Cleo says about #wiggate and why it hurt her so much.

3 Read Twitterlude 5 (pp. 50–51) and outline what the twitterlude consists of.

4 Read Twitterlude 6–9 (pp. 54, 56, 58 and 61). Describe what @INCOGNEGRO's critics do.

5 Read the IRL passages following Twitterludes 6–9 (pp. 55, 57, 59–60 and 62–63). State how Cleo defends herself and how Kara corrects her.

6 Read Twitterlude 10 (pp. 64–65) and summarize in 1–2 sentences what Cleo suggests in her 6th method.

_____

_____

_____

Analysis

7 Examine the language of the tweets in the twitterludes. How does it help form a joint opposition to Cleo?

8 a Compare the role of social media in Cleo's past and present. Use the table below.

Social media in Cleo's past	Social media in Cleo's present

b Compare your answers with a partner.

9 In the table below, you will find a list of things, taken from Twitterlude 10, that Cleo wants Kylie Jenner to experience. Add a sentence of explanation for each of the experiences.

Experience	Explanation
'But I want her to [...] The men in top hats Thick full red lips Tap shoes' (p. 64)[1]	
'I want her to have Aamito's lips and Hottentot Venus' hips Without it being called a trend' (p. 64)[2]	
'I want her to be called blick in the playground Drop lip' (p. 64)[3]	
'I want her to be whipped And put in a box on show for a paying audience' (p. 64)[4]	
'I want her to replace her lip kits for cocoa butter or Vaseline' (p. 64)[5]	
'I want her thighs to be called fat not thick' (p. 64)[6]	
'I want her [...] no-lye relaxer and hotcomb [...] her edges to get burnt [...] boxer braids to turn into canerows' (p. 65)[7]	
'I want her to taste the salt tears [...] at 9 When she is told she's not pretty enough for Cinderella' (p. 65)[8]	

[1-8]: Lee-Jones, Jasmine. *Seven methods of killing Kylie Jenner.* Methuen Drama, 2021, p. 64–65.

Beyond the text

10 a In this section, there is a very quick sequence of twitterludes and short IRL passages. Twitter and real life seem to merge. In small groups, discuss how this could be presented on stage. Consider what messages you would want to bring across with the help of stage design. Make drawings to illustrate your ideas.

   b Speaking Present your ideas in the form of a gallery walk and discuss your ideas with other groups.

B6 The end of the play (IRL and The post-mortem)

Comprehension

1 Read the final section of the play (pp. 69–83) and answer the following questions by ticking the correct answer.

   a Both Kara and Cleo feel that …

      A they should both talk about the past.
      B they now understand each other better.
      C the other should acknowledge her mistakes.
      D they should let go of the hurtful events of the past and move on.

   b Cleo is hurt because Kara …

      A loves her.
      B shaved her head.
      C told her she was gay.
      D officially came out on social media without telling her.

   c Kara brings about a change in Cleo by …

      A finally apologizing for #wiggate.
      B blocking her from her Twitter account.
      C telling her why she came out on her timeline.
      D writing her own tweets to defend Cleo's tweets.

   d In the tweets that follow, Cleo apologizes for her homophobic tweets and says that she …

      A was only joking.
      B is going to apologize to Kylie Jenner.
      C decided not to kill Kylie Jenner after all.
      D is going to delete her tweets about Kylie Jenner.

e Cleo admits that, in reality, she …

    A actually likes Kylie Jenner.
    B knows that she is a violent person.
    C could never imagine killing anyone.
    D has had thoughts about killing Kylie Jenner.

f In the seventh method, Cleo points out that Sarah Baartman …

    A received a proper funeral.
    B was never known by her real name.
    C was eventually sent home to Africa.
    D received money for being looked at by an audience.

g In The post-mortem, Cleo and Kara …

    A swear renewed friendship.
    B realize they cannot forgive each other.
    C once again discuss what happened in the past.
    D bury the symbols of what has hurt them long ago.

2 Briefly summarize Cleo's monologue in the post-mortem. How has Sarah Baartman made her feel differently?

3 With a partner, discuss whether your hypothesis from **B1,2a** was correct.

Analysis

4 Examine this passage with respect to its form, the relationship between the Twittersphere and the IRL passage, the characters' language, the use of memes, etc. Consider the message(s) conveyed by these stylistic choices and how this can be applied to your own life.

5 Cleo's monologue (p. 81–82) can be read like a poem. Analyse how Cleo uses rhetorical devices (simile, metaphor, hyperbole, alliteration, parallelism, etc.) to bring her message across.

Beyond the text

6 a With a partner, turn Cleo's final monologue into a dialogue between Sarah Baartman and Cleo in which Sarah asks Cleo questions and Cleo gives answers based on what was originally said in the monologue. Be prepared to present the dialogue to the class.

   b Speaking Perform your dialogue for the class.

Part C
Post-reading activities

C1 Me and white supremacy *Layla F. Saad*

Read the following excerpts from Layla F. Saad's book *Me and White Supremacy: How to Recognise Your Privilege, Combat Racism and Change the World* and complete the tasks that follow on pp. 168–169.

What is anti-blackness against women?
At the end of 2018, Academy, Emmy and Tony Award-winning actress Viola Davis stepped on stage at the Hollywood Reporter's Women in Entertainment breakfast to accept the Sherry Lansing Leadership
5 Award. During her powerful eleven-minute speech, Davis spoke passionately about what it feels like to be a Black woman in Hollywood:

> 'When I started my production company with my husband … we started it because I got tired of always celebrating movies that didn't have me in it … I don't mean me Viola, I mean me as a Black
> 10 woman … I was tired of seeing the expansive imagination of writers when they wrote the mess, the joy, the beauty, the femininity of white characters. And maybe an hour into the movie, you saw the obligatory Black character just kind of walking into the camera, who had a name – didn't really have to have a name –
> 15 because you know nothing about them. And even when you know something about them, it's always so romanticized. We have to be maternal. We have to be the savior. We have to make that white character feel better.'

Malcom X famously called Black women the most disrespected,
20 unprotected, and neglected people in America. I believe that attitude toward Black women applies outside America too. Black women bring up all kinds of feelings in people with white privilege and non-Black People of Color: fear, awe, envy, disdain, anger, desire, confusion, pity, jealousy, superiority, and more. Black women are either superhumanized
25 and put on pedestals as queens or the strong Black woman, or they are dehumanized and seen as unworthy of the same care and attention as white women. Both superhumanizing and dehumanizing are harmful because, as Davis rightly points out in her speech, they fail to capture Black women in the mess, joy, beauty, and femininity of women of
30 other races.
   Black women are so often underrepresented because they are not seen as women, let alone as people, the same way white women are. Black women are often painted with a broad, monolithic brushstroke that categorizes them into particular stereotypes that rob them of their

00 supremacy: position of having greater power than sb. else
33 monolithic: (here) massive, imposing, hard to change

humanity. In the United States in particular, these stereotypes have arisen out of America's violent slaving history with Black people and Black women in particular. [...]

As Black women, we even have our own class of misogyny directed at us: misogynoir. A term coined by African American feminist scholar, writer and activist Moya Bailey, misogynoir is defined as "the particular brand of hatred directed at Black women in American visual and popular culture." It is a term that describes the place where anti-Black racism and sexism meet, resulting in Black women facing oppression and marginalization under two systems of oppression – white supremacy and patriarchy. Misogynoir reflects the work that law professor, civil rights advocate, and pioneering scholar of critical race theory Kimberlé Crenshaw has led on intersectionality.

How does anti-blackness against black women show up?
Examples of anti-Blackness against women include:
- The derogatory and one-dimensional stereotyping of Black women into categories such as strong, angry, servile, sassy, and so on. [...]
- The underrepresentation of Black women in mainstream media as the protagonist.
- The disdain and disregard toward Black women's style and beauty in the past, which has now been replaced by the appropriation of Black women's style and beauty as desirable – as long as they are placed on bodies that are not Black. [...]

What is anti-blackness against men?
[...] When Black men's sexuality is not feared, it is often fetishized. Black men are often seen as sexual conquests, there to satisfy the white appetite with their allegedly exaggerated genitalia. They are also sometimes seen as a means to an end – a way to produce biracial babies, a way to feel Black (read: edgier, cooler), or a way to anger white parents who would balk at the thought of their white child being in an intimate relationship with a Black man. [...]

From: Saad, Layla F., *Me and White Supremacy: How to Recognise Your Privilege, Combat Racism and Change the World,* Sourcebooks, 2020.

39 misogyny: hatred directed at women
45 marginalization: process or result of making sb. be/feel powerless or less important

Comprehension
1 Summarize the main arguments of the text.

_____

_____

_____

Analysis

2 Compare Layla F. Saad's text with the play *seven methods of killing kylie jenner*. Can some of Saad's arguments be supported by examples from the play?

Beyond the text

3 `Writing` Write a review of the play *seven methods of killing kylie jenner* (→ Info box) in which you comment on the way issues of anti-blackness are addressed. Refer to Layla F. Saad's text 'Me and white supremacy' in your review.

> **Info Writing a text review**
>
> Just like in a **film review** (Info box, p. 154), in a text review, you provide information on a text you have read and express your opinion about it.
>
> To prepare the review, make notes on interesting, positive or negative aspects you notice while reading the text. Find suitable aspects to analyse, e.g. the beginning of the story, the plot development, the characters, the setting, the ending, etc. Take note of chapters or sections in which characters struggle to form their identity. Then structure your ideas. In the introduction of your review, give some basic information on the text and its central theme(s). In the main part, briefly summarize the text's plot and comment on relevant aspects. Finally, give your opinion in the conclusion. State whether you recommend the text, potentially also recommending it for a specific target group. Write from a first-person perspective and use an appropriate register.

4 a In groups, collect ideas on which messages the play brings across with respect to these three topics: ethnic identity, gender and the Twittersphere. How are the topics linked in the play?

b Create a poster visualizing these topics and their interconnectedness. Find or create visuals to add to your posters.

c `Speaking` In a short presentation, present your posters to the class.

d As a class, discuss how this play can contribute to raising awareness of the problems of anti-blackness, discrimination and racism. Include arguments from Layla F. Saad's text in your discussion.

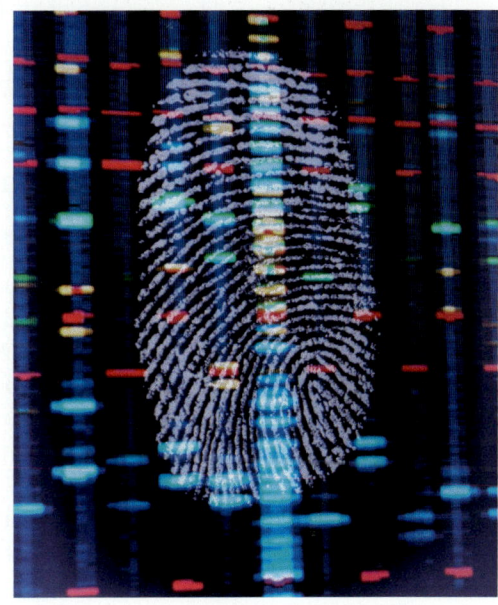

Atonement

Part A
Pre-reading activities

A1 Approaches to the themes of guilt and atonement

1 a In groups of three, describe the pictures above to each other and point out which aspect of guilt is highlighted in each of them. Discuss which one of them best expresses the notion of guilt.

  b (Without a dictionary) Write down your own definition of guilt.

2 a Look up *atonement* in at least three (online) dictionaries. Point out what different domains the word can refer to and explain what these domains have in common.

  b Discuss whether there are crimes that cannot be atoned for.

3 Have a look at the covers of different editions of the novel and of the DVD of the movie, and speculate about the nature and gravity of the crime in *Atonement*.

A2 Unfamiliar words in *Atonement*

1 While reading *Atonement*, you will encounter a number of unfamiliar words and expressions. When coming across such words or expressions, you can try to

| identify **parts** of the word (like roots, prefixes, suffixes) | look for **clues** from the **context** | or | relate the word to **similar words in other languages** |

which might enable you to make an 'educated guess' of the word's meaning. Other strategies are looking it up in a **dictionary**, or simply deciding to ignore it.

a Try to make sense of the underlined words and expressions from an excerpt from *Atonement* by using one of the strategies. Mark your strategy with the respective colour, and write down what you think the expression means.

> A good wedding was an <u>unacknowledged representation</u> of the as yet unthinkable – sexual <u>bliss</u>. In the aisles of country churches and grand city cathedrals, witnessed by a whole society of approving family and friends, her heroines and heroes reached their innocent <u>climaxes</u> and needed to go no further.
> If divorce had presented itself as the <u>dastardly</u> antithesis of all this, it could easily have been <u>cast</u> onto the other <u>pan of the scales</u>, along with betrayal, illness, thieving, assault and <u>mendacity</u>. Instead it showed an unglamorous face of dull complexity and <u>incessant wrangling</u>.
>
> *From: Ian McEwan,* Atonement, *Vintage 2016, p. 9.*

b Apply the strategies to expressions unfamiliar to you in these excerpts.

| **p. 218, 1st par.** ('Some of the vehicles ...' – '... crowbar that was lying nearby.') | **p. 287, 1st par.** |

A3 The author

1 a Do some research on the novel's author, Ian McEwan. Touch upon such domains as the stages of his life, his private and academic background, the themes explored in (at least some of) his novels and the reasons that led him to write *Atonement*.

b Speaking Present your findings in a slide presentation, a poster or an infographic.

Part B
While-reading activities

B1 Part One, chapters 1–3

Comprehension

1 a Fill in the gaps of the following events or ideas from the first three chapters. The events/ideas are not in chronological order.

A It soon turns out that Lola, not Briony, will have the

_____ in the play.

B Cecilia _____ Robbie's help, causing the object to break.

C She feels an urge to _____ of what she has seen.

D Cecilia seeks to fill a valuable _____ with water at a fountain in the garden.

E Witnessing the events, Briony _____ what is happening.

F It is announced that Briony's _____, due to their parents' marital dispute, will be living with the Tallis family for a while.

G She _____ before retrieving the shards from the water.

b Put the sentences from **a** in chronological order. Enter the letter of each sentence in the the table below.

chapter 1	chapter 2	chapter 3

2 a Draw a *sociogram* of the characters mentioned in chapters 1–3 on a sheet of paper. Connect their names with arrows. Add labels to the arrows that provide information about how the characters are related (e.g. sisters, children, friends), how they see each other and how they behave towards each other.

b **Speaking** Present your results in class.

Analysis

3 a In groups, read one of the following excerpts. Analyse Briony's character following these guiding questions:
Which character traits can be deduced from …
 – her activities, actions and behaviour?
 – what we learn about her thoughts?

A Briony, the playwright p. 6, 1st par. ('At the age of eleven …') – p. 8, 1st par. ('… leap into a new form.')	**B Casting the play** p. 11, 3rd par. ('I hate plays …') – **p. 13,** **8th par.** ('… because she was Arabella.')
C Impressions from the rehearsal p. 34, 5th par. ('How marvellous …') – p. 36, 2nd par. ('… she didn't really feel it.')	**D Fountain incident** p. 38, 2nd par. ('What was less comprehensible …') – **p. 40, 7th par.** ('… a story need have.').

b `Speaking` Form new groups and present your results to the students who have worked on the other text passages.

c Using your own words and words from the language help box, name and explain general qualities of Briony's character.

Language help
busy · priggish · conceited · self-conscious · immature · hyperactive · precocious [prɪˈkəʊʃəs] *frühreif* · petulant [ˈpetʃələnt] *mürrisch* · stubborn · callous · thoughtless · bossy · opinionated · imaginative [ɪˈmædʒɪnətɪv] · childish · creative

d `Writing` Later in Part One, the narrator comments that '[a]t this stage in her life Briony inhabited an ill-defined transitional space between nursery and adult worlds which she crossed and recrossed unpredictably' (Ian McEwan, *Atonement*, Vintage, p. 141). In writing, examine this statement using your results from **a** and **c**.

4 a Read the info box on perspective and focalization and clarify questions you may have in class.

Info Perspective and focalization
The **narrator** is the fictitious person or voice telling the story, not to be confused with the **author** creating the whole story. There are **first-person** and **third-person narrators**. A first-person narrator is *per se* subjective and has a limited **point of view**. A third-person narrator can be an **omniscient narrator** [ɒmˈnɪsiənt], having an unlimited point of view and knowing all characters' thoughts and

everything that happens. Or it can be a **personal narrator** whose knowledge is limited to the thoughts and perceptions of one of the story's characters.

The term (internal) **focalization** – coined by the linguist Gérard Genette – is very useful for describing the changing perspectives in *Atonement*. Focalization can be understood as the restriction of the narrator's perspective to one character, the focalizer. The **focalizer** is not the narrator of the story but the person through whose eyes the narrator – and, thus, the reader – sees the story.

b Examine the author's narrative technique in two excerpts either from chapters 1 and 3 or from chapter 2. Mind the following guiding questions:
  – Who is the *character* that is being focalized?
  – What *kind of language* is used by the narrator?
  – What *kind of information* is given by the narrator?
  – What *effect* does the information and language have on you as a reader?

Chapters 1 and 3	Chapter 2
p. 12, last par. – p. 13, 1st par.	p. 22, last par. – p. 23, 1st par.
p. 39, last par. – p. 40, 1st par.	p. 26, 12th par. ('He looked away again …') – p. 27, 3rd par. ('… wrong-footing her whenever he could')

Beyond the text

5 Discuss whether the first three chapters of *Atonement* are motivating enough for the reader to read on.

6 On the right, you will find some topics and themes in *Atonement*.
  a From the topics on the right (or possibly others that come to your mind), choose four that are important in chapters 1–3. Make brief notes about each of them on a cue card.
  b Speaking In a short presentation, describe and explain your ideas to the class.
  c Speaking Discuss which of these topics is the most important one in chapters 1–3.

perspective

truth/memory

guilt

social class

literature

war

B2 Part One, chapters 4–14

Comprehension

1 Put the brief summaries of chapters 4–14 (p. 175) in the correct order. While doing so, spot and correct a mistake in three of the summaries.

Statement	Chapter
A Robbie reflects on his feelings for Cecilia, writes her a letter and hands it over to Briony. He then realizes that he has given Briony a draft that ends with an obscene postscript.	
B On the island, Briony discovers Lola, who has obviously fallen victim to a sexual assault. She barely sees the silhouette of a man leaving, yet determines that this person must have been Robbie.	
C After Briony has reported her version of the incident to the police, Robbie is arrested when he returns to the house with Lola.	
D Emily is absorbed in her thoughts. She talks to her husband on the phone until Leon and others, in distress, come rushing into the house.	
E Leon Tallis and Paul Marshall arrive. Cecilia is angry with Leon for having invited Paul to dinner.	
F During the family dinner, many slightly aggressive remarks are passed. Briony finds a note from her boy cousins that reveals that they have run away.	
G Briony starts to sympathize with Lola and tells her about the letter. She observes Robbie and Cecilia making love in the nursery.	
H In her bedroom, Emily contemplates the situation, her life, and her family.	
I Paul meets the cousins who have started to feel homesick and restless.	
J Briony gives Robbie's letter to Cecilia. Cecilia knows that Briony must have read it.	
K Attacking the bushes, Briony is play-acting being an Olympic athlete. Robbie and Paul drive past her.	

2 Complete your sociogram (see **B1,2a**) by adding information about new and already familiar characters.

Analysis

3 The theme of social class is brought into focus in the final chapters of Part One, especially in connection with Robbie.
   a Name and explain aspects that determine social class in Germany today.
   b Read the info box on the next page about social class in Britain.

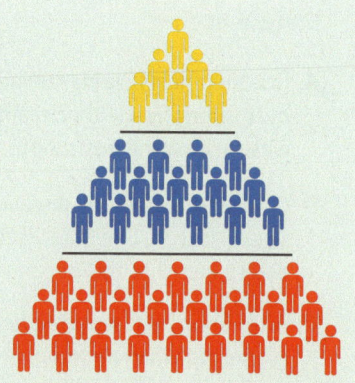

Info Social class in Britain

For many centuries, British society had a rigid class system based on socioeconomic differences, which made it very difficult for people to move up classes. There were three major classes in British society: the upper class, the middle

5   class, and the working class. While the class structure started to become more flexible in the second half of the 20th century, social class still plays an important role in determining a person's identity in modern-day British society. The **upper class** traditionally included the nobility and

10 families who could trace their heritage back many centuries. They owned most of the land and most of the industries. Their wealth enabled them to live privileged and prosperous lives. They held powerful positions in politics and the military. Their children received a private education and often attended one of the two most prestigious universities in the country: Oxford or

15 Cambridge.

Working class people, in contrast, owned and earned little and had to work in hard and often unskilled jobs, either as tenant farmers, servants or in the factories of the cities. In between was the **middle class**, which included a wide range of skilled, managerial and professional workers. The upper middle class had acquired their money through some form

20 of business, often in banking or law. They enjoyed many of the lifestyle privileges of the upper class, but fewer social privileges.

'Old money', i.e., wealth passed down through the family over generations, was traditionally more respected than 'new money', i.e., wealth acquired more recently through trade and industry.

c Discuss what social class the following characters belong to.

Paul Marshall

Danny Hardman

Jack Tallis

Grace Turner

Leon Tallis

Robbie Turner

d Focusing on Robbie's relationship with the Tallises, examine Cecilia's, Robbie's and Emily's perceptions of social class.

Cecilia	Robbie	Emily
p. 27, 3rd par.	p. 79, 2nd par. – p. 80, 1st par. ('… would be gone.') p. 86, 3rd par. ('He was without social unease …')	p. 64, 2nd par. – p. 65, 1st par. ('… spoken of in lowered voices.') p. 151, 2nd par. – p. 152, 1st par. ('… plenty of good had come already.')

e Writing In an argumentative essay, discuss whether Robbie Turner was 'doomed to fail' from the very beginning.

Beyond the text

4 a Prepare questions you would like to ask Jack Tallis,
Robbie Turner and Briony about the events of Part One.

b `Speaking` In groups, choose different members to enact these
characters. In 'hot chair' interrogations, the characters answer
their classmates' questions.

B3 Part Two

Comprehension

1 Create a timeline with the most important events of Part Two, taking
Robbie's imprisonment as a starting point.

Analysis

2 a Characterize Robbie Turner by choosing adjectives that describe
him best from the box below. Give a short summary of the
relevant passages from the text in your characterization.

> brave · independent · compassionate · sensitive · fainthearted · decisive · hesitant ·
> rebellious · weak · melancholy · hateful · calm

b Reread pages 192–195 closely and describe Robbie's social status.

c The narrator refers to Robbie only by his surname. Describe the
resulting effect.

3 As Robbie reflects on his past, he imagines confronting Briony.

a Scan pages 227 ff. for evidence for how Robbie feels about Briony.

b `Writing` Write a monologue in which Robbie tells Briony his
thoughts and feelings.

Beyond the text

4 a Search the web for more information on the British army's
evacuation of Dunkirk in 1940.

b Based on the information you found in **a**, explain why 'Dunkirk' is
still a part of Britain's public memory.

c Use the information from **a** and speculate why McEwan chose
Dunkirk instead of another theatre of war as the setting of Part Two.

d `Viewing` Watch the Dunkirk scene [1:02:50–1:07:50]
of Joe Wright's film version of *Atonement*.

– Choose a still from the scene that impressed you.
Present it to the class and explain your choice.

– While watching, take notes on visual and other devices
used in the scene (music, editing, perspective, etc.).
Analyse their effect on the viewer and evaluate whether
the scene is a good adaptation of the passage in the novel.

B4 Part Three

Comprehension

1 Tick the correct answer for each item and find a short quote
  (5–7 words) in the text to support it.

  a There is a growing feeling of unease at the hospital because ...

		page:
A they are going to be evacuated.		
B the probationers do not have the required skills.		quote:
C there are not enough trained nurses.		
D an influx of injured soldiers is expected.		

  b The work climate among the nurses at the hospital is characterized
  by ...

		page:
A mutual respect.		
B humanistic principles.		quote:
C military-like discipline.		
D Christian charity.		

  c Briony's relationship to her parents can be described as ...

		page:
A distant.		
B hostile.		quote:
C intimate.		
D affectionate.		

  d The magazine *Horizon* tells Briony that ...

		page:
A she is not talented enough.		
B they will print her story in the next issue.		quote:
C they are only interested in war-related texts.		
D her story lacks development.		

  e As Briony tends to the wounded soldiers, she realizes that ...

		page:
A she would rather be in Scotland and work as a land-girl.		
B war has changed her a lot.		quote:
C Robbie could be among them.		
D the human body is fragile.		

f When Briony appears at Lola's wedding, …

   A Lola is happy to see her cousin.
   B Lola does not notice her.
   C Lola can hardly conceal her disapproval.
   D Paul Marshall casts her a knowing look.

page:

quote:

g After Lola's wedding, Briony speaks to Robbie and Cecilia. Briony promises to …

   A confront Paul Marshall and Lola.
   B publish a rectification of her testimony.
   C retract her testimony.
   D never speak about the incident again.

page:

quote:

Analysis

2 Analyse how a feeling of guilt manifests in Briony and how she deals with it.

> For examples see pages 275–276, 279, 285, 288–289, 312, 339.

3 Discuss whether Briony has matured and become more empathetic. Name examples from the text.

Beyond the text

4 `Writing` During the night before her wedding, Lola is lying awake and thinking about whether she is doing the right thing. Write her interior monologue (→ Info box, p. 36). Take into consideration the following aspects and what might have happened since the events at the Tallis Estate.

| class and money | hopes and fears | age and innocence |

B5 London, 1999

Comprehension

1 Decide whether the statements in the table on p. 180 are true (T) or false (F). Back up your answers with evidence from the text.

	T/F	Evidence (page number and short paraphrase)
A Briony has been diagnosed with Alzheimer's disease.		
B At the Imperial War Museum, Briony avoids running into Paul Marshall and Lola.		
C Briony attached little importance to military details in her novel.		
D The reader learns that Briony has never been married.		
E Briony leaves for an overnight trip to her former home where she is going to celebrate her 75th birthday.		
F The Tallis Estate is now a guest house called Tillney's hotel.		
G Before her birthday dinner, *The Trials of Arabella* are performed by her family.		
H In her room, Briony decides to publish her novel before losing her memory.		
I Briony reveals that she never visited Robbie and Cecilia, who both died during the war.		
J Briony decided to let the lovers live on in her novel to hide her own guilt.		

Analysis

2 a Create a chart that describes the relationships between author(s), narrator(s) and focalizer(s), and the narrated events.

b Present your findings in class.

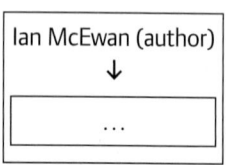

Ian McEwan (author)
↓
...

180

3 Briony calls it the 'least of [her] offences against veracity' (p. 356) that, in her narrative, she has worked in only one hospital while in reality she has worked in three, indicating that her description of events has not always been completely accurate.

  a Form four groups. Each group focuses on one part of the novel and assesses the reliability of the information given. Take into consideration what we have learned in 'London, 1999' about events described in Parts One to Three. In the box below, you can find possible reasons for a narrator's unreliability.

> immaturity · limited knowledge/perspective · mental defense mechanisms · mental illness · character traits · narrator's involvement in the events that are described

Example (Part One): Briony comforts Lola after the assault. She acts as a witness and accuses Robbie even though she cannot have seen him (ch. 13). Her false testimony is based on her limited perspective and prejudices she holds against Robbie.

  b Discuss why McEwan filters the narrative through different characters' points of view instead of choosing just Briony as a first-person narrator (→ Info box, p. 173).

Beyond the text

4 Writing Read the following excerpt from a book review of *Atonement* and comment on it.

Why I hate the ending of *Atonement*
[...] The problem for me is that Briony is actually engaging in exactly the same type of behavior that created the whole mess in the first place. Instead of trying to understand a more complicated or ambiguous reality, she opts for a romanticized, tidy fiction. Even though the ending of her novel is an attempt to make things right, it still shields Briony from the guilt of her original mistake and keeps her audience from knowing how severe the consequences were. To me, this represents an utter failure on Briony's part – even as she attempts to atone for her mistake, she cannot resist sanitizing reality so that it fits her own desires. [...]
From: Justin Heinzekehr, 'Why I hate the ending of Atonement', *The Book List*, February 19, 2014.

Part C
Post-reading activities

C1 Britishness and social mobility

1 Collect aspects that you associate with 'Britishness'.

2 The term *social mobility* refers to the transition from one social class to another, either within an individual's lifetime or over generations.

   a Name examples of *social mobility* of different characters in *Atonement*.

   b Collect information about Britain's current social mobility crisis.

   c Read the following text by Peter Wilby. Point out the evidence John Goldthorpe provides to disprove the assumption that there is a close connection between social mobility and education in Britain.

The expert in social mobility who says education cannot make it happen

[W]hy does [John Goldthorpe] insist that conventional wisdom about social mobility and education's role in it is wrong? In a recent book, Social Mobility and Education in Britain, written jointly with Erzsébet Bukodi, a Nuffield colleague, he distinguishes between absolute and relative
5 mobility. Absolute mobility is your chance of ending up in a different social class from the one you were born into. That is around 80% and has been remarkably consistent for at least a century; if anything, Britain has slightly more mobility than other European countries. But the movement is often small: from class 2 to 1, say, or from class 5 to 6.

10 Relative mobility is different. That is your chance, if you started in, say, class 6 or 7, of making it to, say, class 1 or 2 compared with those who started at the top. Here, if you start at the bottom, you are many times less likely to make it to the top than somebody born there. That remains as true as ever, say Bukodi and Goldthorpe. Neither grammar
15 schools nor comprehensives made any difference either way. [...]

Even if children from the top social classes fail at school, they often fall on their feet. The majority of men with the double handicaps of low qualifications and socially disadvantaged backgrounds end up in the working class and only 16% become professionals. But of similarly
20 qualified men from the most advantaged homes, only a fifth sink to the working class and nearly half stay in the managerial and professional class.

How do they manage that? 'Some get jobs in a parent's business. Others in the service sector, selling to people from similar social backgrounds: high-grade travel firms, marque car dealers, high-grade
25 hotels and restaurants, fashion shops.' [...]

Can education be made more effective in countering the advantages of the already advantaged? 'I would support lotteries for allocating

9 class 2 to 1: Goldthorpe established the categorization of British society into seven social classes ('1' being the highest)
14 grammar school: elite secondary school, often privately owned
15 comprehensive (school): regular state-funded school

secondary school places,' he says. 'And to even things up, you could give disadvantaged parents vouchers to buy private tuition for their children.'

38 golden age (of sth.): (here) 1950s and 1960s

30   Abolishing private schools, he says, wouldn't make much difference, except at elite levels of the civil service, the judiciary and so on, because it involves such a small proportion of children.

But before meddling further with education, Goldthorpe argues, governments should develop an industrial strategy that creates more
35 good management jobs and also upgrade welfare services such as old people's care which, instead of providing mostly unskilled and low-paid jobs, could be turned into a profession. We need to get back to the golden age, he and Bukodi argue, when jobs that offered a secure, regular income and prospects of career progression steadily increased.
40 Instead, we've moved in the opposite direction to the insecure, dead-end work of the gig economy.

From: Peter Wilby, 'The expert in social mobility who says education cannot make it happen', *theguardian.com,* 17.03.2020.

3 On the basis of Goldthorpe's findings and ideas, discuss ways to enhance upward social mobility.

C2 Guilt and innocence

1 a Work with a partner. Discuss which factors define crimes, offenses and mistakes. Consider aspects such as age, intent or consequences.
b Fill in the following grid. Use expressions from **a** and the language help box on the next page. Many different answers are possible.

Example of mistake, offense, crime	Possible effect(s) on offender	Way(s) of atonement and/or punishment
		apologizing
drunken driver injures person in a car accident		
not paying taxes on your income (by accident vs. deliberately)		
	unbearable feelings of guilt	

Language help
apologize for sth. · atone for sth. · make up for sth. · make amends for sth. · repent (for) sth. · reconcile · atonement · (be consumed with, be racked with, suffer from) guilt · burden of guilt · (get one's) comeuppance · (show genuine/sincere/true) repentance · (express, feel deep/great) regret · (be filled with, be stricken with, express deep/genuine) remorse · (strive for, seek) reconciliation

c Analyse to what extent the characters below are to blame for the way events unfold in the novel and rank them according to the severity of their guilt.

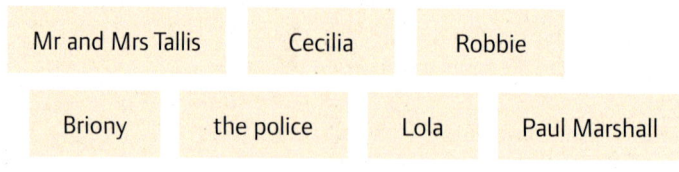

Mr and Mrs Tallis	Cecilia	Robbie

Briony	the police	Lola	Paul Marshall

2 At the end of the novel, Briony is convinced that being forgiven is 'an impossible task'.
   a Reread p. 371 and name the reasons Briony gives for her inability to atone.
   b Writing Write a comment in which you examine whether Briony is right in her assertion.

C3 Perception(s) of reality

1 a Read the info box below about *historiographic metafiction* and write down a one-sentence definition of the term.
   b Create a poster about *Atonement* as an example of *historiographic metafiction* referring to the metafictive strategies mentioned in the info box and other aspects of your reading experience.

Info Historiographic metafiction
The term *historiographic metafiction* was first introduced by the Canadian literary critic Linda Hutcheon in the 1980s. The word *historiographic* translates as 'writing of history', while *metafiction* means 'writing about writing'. The narrative in *metafictive* novels is generally self-reflexive and reminds the readers of the constructed and artificial quality of fiction. Metafictive texts use strategies such as unreliable, obtrusive or multiple narrators, disruptions of time and space, insertion of other text types, and typographic experimentation, all of which can draw attention to how a narrative is created. It might lead readers to question the idea of a coherent story and characters' stable identities. In *historiographic* metafiction, these strategies make readers aware of the way reality ('history') is filtered through storytelling, or how the past is constructed through narrative.